This book belongs to:

How to Decorate

AN INSPIRING AND PRACTICAL HANDBOOK

SHANNON FRICKE

PHOTOGRAPHY BY PRUE RUSCOE

POTTER STYLE
NEW YORK

INTRODUCTION
IX

GETTING STARTED
3

LAYER ONE
DISCOVERING YOUR
DECORATING STORY
13

Contents

LAYER TWO
CREATING YOUR CONCEPT
27

LAYER THREE
WORKING WITH SPACE
39

LAYER FOUR
SHAPING YOUR BACKDROP
55

LAYER FIVE
BECOMING FRIENDS
WITH COLOUR
79

LAYER SIX
BRINGING IN THE
FURNITURE
101

Introduction

We can't always change the wrapping of a building – but we do have control over the look and feel of what goes on within its four walls. If you want to create a home you love living in, one that reflects you, your life and your passions, but you don't know how to begin, then this book is for you.

I was inspired to write this book by the decorating workshops I run in my studio in country Australia. These workshops draw women (men are also very welcome but never seem to come!) from all walks of life, from places near and far, with different ways of living and different points of view. At the heart of the workshop days lies a common goal shared by every woman who steps through the front door – to be creative.

Decorating is a form of creativity, an opportunity to express our unique style of seeing things in a legitimate way. I say legitimate because sometimes the world can look upon the act of being creative as a pastime, an indulgence of sorts, for those who have too much time on their hands and little else in the way of 'real work'. What a shame, I say, that we don't give the act of being creative the credit it so definitely deserves. Creativity in any form is a clear window into our soul, into who we are and how we see things. It inspires us to know ourselves – from our head all the way through to our heart. The experience of using our minds, our hands and our inner spirit in tandem is an opportunity to achieve a kind of peace. To just be . . . How lovely to have such a chance in this crazy, fast-moving, ever-evolving world!

The lovely thing about engaging with decorating as a form of creativity is that the outcome can be both functional and beautiful. It's easier to navigate the footprint of a well-decorated house, and all who live among its virtues feel its influence on an aesthetic and spiritual level. And on top of all this, good decoration adds value to the property, which for some people is reason enough. For me, however, the true joy of decorating, the heart of the experience, will always lie in the act of creativity itself.

A decorating workshop in a book

The decorating workshops I run are not only a great way for me to impart my own creative point of view but also to be inspired by the creativity of the gorgeous women who share the day with me. We have such a great time, and I wish you could all come along to share in the experience.

I've written and designed these pages as a kind of workshop in a book — taking you through the creative process, the nitty gritty of what you need to think about and the tools you'll need to embark on the journey of decorating your own home. It's a myth that you need endless funds to live in a well-decorated home. Of course those with money can choose from a wider pool of fittings and furniture, but expensive things don't make for a thoughtful interior. For that you need passion and thought! And with patience and a certain degree of focus, we all have it in us to infuse passion into our home.

This book takes on decorating one layer at a time. It's designed for decorating enthusiasts of all kinds, but particularly the decorating novice — those who love the idea of creating a beautifully decorated home but are unsure where to begin. Here you'll find all the information you need to begin to shape your space.

To ensure that you make the best choices for your particular space, it's important to read the whole book before you make any final decisions on your colour and furnishing palette. Try to be patient, take your time and have fun on the way — it's better to get it right first go than spend the money and realise your scheme isn't quite right for your space.

Thanks!

With all my heart, I'd like to say a big thank you to all the lovely women who've made it to one of my How to Decorate workshops. I've met inspiring women with extraordinary stories, women whose lives have helped shape my own life and creativity. There's something quite marvellous about a group of women holed up together in a room, sharing their creative visions. I hope, through reading this book, you'll feel the same connection from the comfort of your own home. And I hope these pages will inspire you to embark on your own creative journey.

Happy decorating!

Decorating is a form of creativity, an opportunity to express your unique way of seeing things. While putting your creative point of view out there can be daunting at first, once you take the leap, it can also be exhilarating and a little addictive.

Inspiring women who love to decorate

These are shots from my How to Decorate workshops, which I hold regularly in my cottage studio in New South Wales. Small groups of women get together and spend a day getting creative and playing with all aspects of decorating, from colour to room plans and everything in between.

If you'd like to participate in one of my workshops, visit my website, **shannonfricke.com**.

Getting started

To decorate successfully you need a space to work and think in, one that is dedicated to your decorative endeavour. Here are some thoughts on how to create a working space of your own.

I feel blessed to have a dedicated workspace, which I've shaped in the image of my own creativity and sense of style. While moving from the city to a small country town has been extraordinarily inspiring on one level, it can also be quite isolating. In terms of a working life, taking yourself out of the action is always a risk. Deep in my heart I knew that moving to more open, greener spaces was a calling of sorts – and you should never ignore a calling! But to survive doing what I love to do in a small town, I was going to have to seed my own little creative hub, a place that would draw likeminded enthusiasts into my orbit. My studio was born from this desire to remain connected; the decorating workshops I hold in my space are both a lovely manifestation of my yearning and a great way to remain in the loop.

In these images you're seeing my studio in its best light – it doesn't always look so organised, of course! At its heart, a studio is a place of work, a place of ideas and experimentation, a place to bring together the bits and bobs that inspire you and that together represent your own point of view.

I draw upon so many different elements in forming my own creative vision. Sometimes this means my studio is filled to the brim with products; swatches of fabrics; sample paint pots of all shapes and sizes; paintbrushes; drop sheets; vases filled with flowers, branches and twigs; and cardboard boxes piled high with cushion inserts or filled with wallpaper rolls. In short, it's crazy-messy with stuff. And this, after all, is the reality of creating room schemes, developing product lines and styling photographic shoots. That said, while it's of core importance for a workspace to inspire creativity, being able to order the space at the end of a working day is vital for clarity of thought and ideas.

Setting up your own studio space

How you organise your own space very much depends on how you need it to work for you. I have a library of books and magazines that I need to access easily every day; the images and ideas they contain are the basis for important research and even a potential room scheme. I like to organise my library in open cubbyholes so that I can easily see each magazine's issue date or each book's title.

My fabric swatches are colour coded and stored in clear plastic boxes, each of which is divided into smaller sections. My fabric books are hung from wall hooks, which means not only that they provide some decoration for my walls but also that I have quick access to the books I use most often. It's important to keep your most used fabric books out in the open, but it's equally important to keep your least used in a closed cupboard (filed by brand and category), so your walls and desk don't become overloaded with detail or clutter. It's a good idea to rotate your fabrics and wallpaper books, so you're inspired to delve into materials you might not otherwise think to use.

Decorate your workspace in a way that motivates you to work. For me, a healthy balance of clutter and order is just the thing, but depending on the kind of person you are, you could work better in a more utilitarian space, one with little adornment or detail that could be an annoying distraction. The key to creating a successful workplace is to read your habits and listen to what they tell you about yourself.

A clean, non-dusty space is a must; my studio has a good dose of cleaning every week, particularly because here in the country we tend to be surrounded by a lot of grass and mud! While having a large studio is a lovely indulgence, it's by no means mandatory. Your studio may be a simple desk pushed into the corner of the living room, or a laptop perched on top of the coffee table or a corner table in your favourite café (which has been my nook for much of the process of writing this book).

The key is that the environment you choose inspires you to work within it. It really is as simple as that.

Fashion your workspace exactly as you need it to operate for you. Always underpin it with a degree of order, and then layer it as colourfully and creatively as you like. You want to create a space that inspires you to work, after all!

You are your own client

There are two ways to decorate a home: the quick way and the slow way. Buying furniture quickly to fill a space will indeed fill the space, but it will probably leave you with a mix of disparate pieces that don't hang together and don't allow the room to flow. This is not the way to a pretty home! The slow way (in other words, following the steps laid out for you in these pages) can be excruciating at times, I admit, particularly if you're the impatient type. But if your aim is to create a home with vision and flow, then it's important to follow the same steps a decorator would to create a home for a client.

In this case, *you* are the client! By taking the slow way and being disciplined in your decision-making, you are sure to create a well-rounded interior you'll love and that will last the distance. As you grow more confident in your decorating abilities, you'll find that it takes much less time to create an interior. And in the process, you'll have learnt a new skill and refined your vision. For that alone, it's well worth the journey.

The most inspiring homes I've ever stepped into are those that have evolved over time, so I always recommend taking it slowly and being patient when decorating your own home. Savour every stage and every decision along the way.

The tools of the decorating trade

Here are your must-have decorator tools:

FOLDER A ring binder with labelled plastic sleeves is ideal for ordering and organising your mood board inspiration.

CAMERA To take photographs of anything and everything, of any inspiration you see around you, and before, during and after photographs of the spaces you're transforming.

BUILDER'S TAPE MEASURE For a quick measure of a space, a piece of furniture or a floor rug, invest in the longest tape you can find that will still fit neatly in your bag. It's a good idea to have one for your handbag and one for your toolbox.

SCANNER For scanning magazine cuttings, other printed material and fabrics, so you can create your mood boards and plans on your computer.

SWATCHES Have swatches of paints, laminates, carpets, fabrics, tiles, trims and wallpaper in various colours at hand to aid in your decision-making.

ARTIST'S PAINTS AND PENCILS To develop a relationship with colour. The trick of using paints and pencils is to play, play, play.

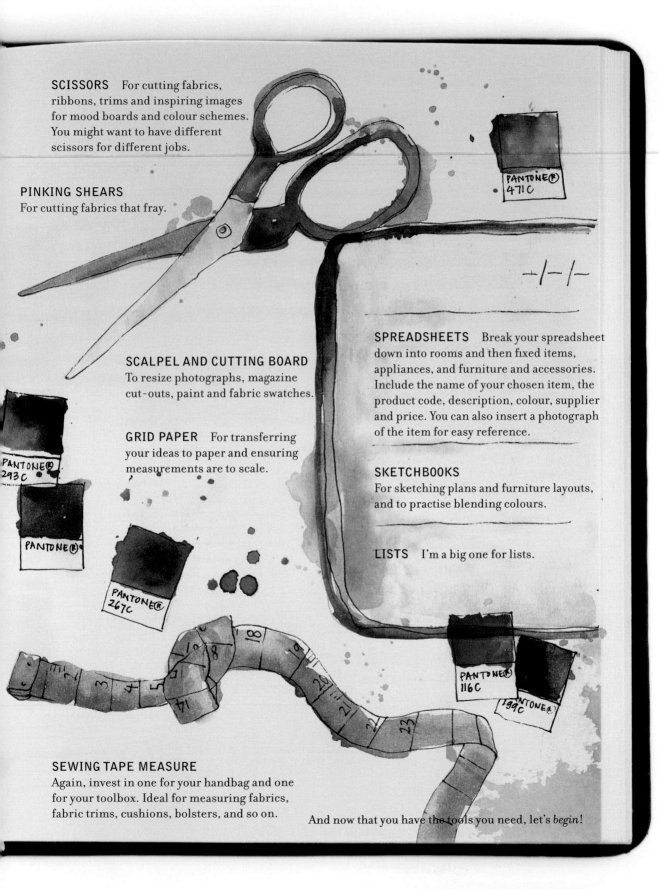

SCISSORS For cutting fabrics, ribbons, trims and inspiring images for mood boards and colour schemes. You might want to have different scissors for different jobs.

PINKING SHEARS
For cutting fabrics that fray.

PANTONE® 471C

SCALPEL AND CUTTING BOARD
To resize photographs, magazine cut-outs, paint and fabric swatches.

GRID PAPER For transferring your ideas to paper and ensuring measurements are to scale.

PANTONE® 293C

PANTONE®

PANTONE® 267C

SPREADSHEETS Break your spreadsheet down into rooms and then fixed items, appliances, and furniture and accessories. Include the name of your chosen item, the product code, description, colour, supplier and price. You can also insert a photograph of the item for easy reference.

SKETCHBOOKS
For sketching plans and furniture layouts, and to practise blending colours.

LISTS I'm a big one for lists.

SEWING TAPE MEASURE
Again, invest in one for your handbag and one for your toolbox. Ideal for measuring fabrics, fabric trims, cushions, bolsters, and so on.

PANTONE® 116C

PANTONE® 199C

And now that you have the tools you need, let's *begin*!

LAYER ONE

Discovering your decorating story

Telling your own decorating story

Like all forms of creativity, decorating a home is the opportunity to tell a story, to express a point of view and ultimately to realise a vision. The most evocative interiors are those that embody the essence, heart and energy of their inhabitants – they are layered and filled with memories, life and stories. They don't subscribe to one particular style; rather, they use the elements of decorating – the combination of furniture, colours, patterns and textures – to tell their story. A home decorated with the individual or family in mind can act as a kind of support system, giving its inhabitants a happy core within which to relax, live and breathe.

While I'm all for the excitement, energy and 'newness' that fashion can give us, I can't help but feel that when a home is decorated for fashion's sake alone it's a missed opportunity. After all, fashion is so fleeting, and doesn't do much to build a thoughtful and lasting aesthetic. Fashion can leave us perpetually dissatisfied, forever on the hunt for the newest style, dissuading us from settling on a longer lasting vision. Of course, infusing elements of fashion helps keep an interior fresh, but interiors shaped with a vision or 'story' in mind are always the most enduring and compelling.

Whoever I'm decorating for, I always begin by constructing the story of the space and the people living in it. I find this the best way to humanise a space and give it a personality. Unearthing your story isn't easy, I admit. We're complex creatures with many facets, elements and stories. But once you begin to take note of your life, the places you love and the things that make you smile, you'll see a thread or a pattern emerging that will form the basis of your decorating story. This process becomes a little trickier when you have to consider not just your story, but also those of the people who share your life. The key is finding common threads and using them as your starting point.

From story to design

Once you have your story in place, you can begin to piece together the decorating puzzle, matching that story with colour, texture and spatial configurations. The aim is to elicit some ideas and watch as they begin to flower. Begin loosely by sifting back through your life — going through old photo albums, memorabilia, memories — and asking yourself these questions:

1   **MEMORIES**   What lovely memories resonate most intensely for you? Perhaps it's a time abroad, travelling through richly textured cultures. Maybe it's holidays by the beach, swimming in azure waters or trekking through the Himalayas — a muted landscape punctuated by the bright colours of the locals' traditional dress — or a special get-together with family and friends, or your childhood home. Think back to places you've been — or think forward to places you hope to go. What does the landscape look like? What's going on there?

2   **FEELINGS**   Why do these experiences resonate for you? What do you love about them? How do they make you feel?

3   **THREADS**   Can you identify a thread, emotion or energy that exists through all your experiences? It could be a colour, a type of celebration, a texture even. Once you sense the thread, you can use it as a framework for your story. Perhaps it's a love of people, of human connection, that stirs you the most. At the other extreme, solitude may be what you crave. Or a connection to nature or a desire for glamour. Identifying the energy you need to live in will help when making decisions about your space, palette and textures.

Look to the things around you — whether they're bric-a-brac or memories — as the first step towards building your own design profile. Studying the things you love is an important first step, as they give great insight into the kinds of colours, textures and shapes you're drawn to most.

My story

I love open spaces and a connection to nature. For me, being surrounded by nature helps me to breathe, which in turn enables me to think more clearly and to focus. My family is a high-energy one — we're always busy, busy, busy, even when sitting still — and so I like to counterbalance this craziness by evoking a sense of calm in my surroundings, which keeps everyone on an even keel.

The beach is a favourite outing for us on weekends — and we particularly love calm seas with a turquoise cast, and white sandy beaches. While we love elements of contemporary life and the freedom that the modern world brings, we also have a healthy respect for old-world places and traditions — we'll always choose to live in an old house rather than a new one, as long as we can give that old house a little freshen-up! Houses that can't be moulded, that are stuck in the past, are not for us. We're an optimistic bunch at our core and won't be held back by antiquated traditions that no longer work.

We love to travel — and are constantly inspired by other cultures and how they live, their routines and traditions. We celebrate differences in cultures and love to infuse the best elements of other cultures into our daily life: food from Greece, the decorative pattern in a Turkish rug, the French love of order with a twist of English eccentricity, the American ability to entertain, all thrown together in a laid-back, Australian way.

My home

I'd like to think that how my home is decorated is a true embodiment of all the elements I outlined in my story. We live in an old weatherboard house (built in the early 1900s) surrounded by grassy hills and misty valleys. The house sits on top of a hill, and sometimes I feel as though I'm living in a cloud. I love this combination of green, blue–grey and white.

Green is such a calming colour, which is exactly what we need to counteract our busy family energy. Soft blue–grey and white have a similar sedative effect. Where to apply the white was easy enough — I'm a white-wall girl and love crisp white joinery and furniture. Blue–grey was just the colour for the old yellowing pine floorboards on the verandas. Choosing the right green proved to be the trickiest part. Mint green is too soft and girly — not a great palette for the boys of the house. Sage green is too dusty — not pure and clear enough for me. And the house, while a little rundown, has a certain majesty to it — I think of it as matriarchal.

In my colour-palette travels, I came across a beautiful peacock blue–green and fell in love with it at first sight. This green ticked all the boxes: not too pretty, not too masculine, with a kind of regal aspect that was sophisticated and reminded me of old-world country houses. Perfect!

Once I'd set the palette, it was a matter of filling in the gaps and *realising* the palette. The decoration of the house is a balance of all the (sometimes contradictory) things I love. There's space and order, but enough knick-knacks to prevent it from feeling bare or barren. Although the house is old-world, most of my furniture has a modern edge, with clean lines and streamlined shapes. Even the mid-century pieces (the 1960s George Nelson Bubble Lamps and Richard Schultz Petal Tables) are modern and geometric in essence.

I also couldn't help but infuse some folly into the interior. I love a space that doesn't take itself too seriously, and Florence Broadhurst wallpapers never fail to deliver in this way. Once I chose her Shadow Floral in Dusty Turquoise, it became the backbone to the palette. In the same way, the Cole & Son Palm Leaves wallpaper in the bedroom adds a laid-back islander flavour with a glamorous edge.

My home, for better or worse, is a true reflection of what we love and how we like to live. It's lovely to look at but comfortable and homey at the same time. It provides us with an enormous amount of pleasure and feels like a part of the family – which is exactly as I love things to be.

Our nest encapsulates the things I love and how we like to live as a family, and the ideal complement to the personality of the house itself. A harmonious interior blends all of these elements equally.

EXERCISE:
Use your life as a creative springboard

Understanding what you love and how you like to live is an integral first step in decorating. The key is to create a space that fits you and your lifestyle, after all. Take the time to review yourself and the people who share your home by following these steps. You might be surprised at what you find out about yourself once you start probing!

1   **CONNECT WITH WHAT YOU LOVE**   Write down in a workbook or journal the things that resonate with you the most: places you (or the people around you) love, experiences that have shaped who you are, jewellery you're drawn to, fabrics that make you smile. The list can be as short or as long as you wish — there are no rights or wrongs here. This is your story, so tell it as it is.

2   **FIND THE THEMES**   Look over your list and see if you can pick out the dominant themes. You might find that there's a colour theme: perhaps the green grass of the countryside appears as the backdrop to many of your experiences; or your love of black-and-white photography indicates that a monochromatic palette would be best for you; or if this seems too harsh, then perhaps one tone on another tone is more your speed. Yours might be a more decorative or textural theme: a diamond brooch indicates a love of detail with a touch of old-world bling; an old kimono illustrates a love of patterning (in a simple organic shape), bright colour and soft flowing fabrics. Or yours might even be an ambient theme: a love of long, lazy days at the beach could indicate the need to be surrounded by soft textures and a fresh, sunny palette.

3   **MAKE NOTES**   Write down the themes that best represent what you love. Seeing your thoughts on paper will make them appear more concrete and easier to wrangle and understand. Use your list as your creative manifesto, the backbone of your decorative palette, and keep it in your mind. Keep your workbook with you throughout the decorating process so you can refer back to your list. This will keep your vision clear as you navigate your way through the decorating options.

4   DO YOUR RESEARCH   With your broad themes in mind (glamorous, relaxed, tone-on-tone, beach, and so on), start looking for specific inspiration by trawling through magazines and collecting pictures that represent what you're drawn to. File these in clear plastic sleeves in your ring binder, organising them into clear labelled sections, such as colour, furniture, lighting, fabrics, wallpaper and flooring. This process could take you months or you might find that an afternoon dedicated to the task is all you need.

5   FIND THE COMMON THREAD   Now analyse your pictures as you did your story in step 2. This can be the tricky part — I often find that clients diligently collect pictures they love and divide them into clear sections, but then fall down when they're asked to analyse their choices. If you take the time to look at your pictures analytically, you'll find common threads running through them all. Rarely does a client collect pictures without a thread, even if it's a slightly tenuous one to begin with. You might find that there's a common colour or pattern. Perhaps a love of clean lines will become apparent or a particular style in all the materials — industrial concrete flooring; soft, flowing fabrics; well-placed Hamptons-inspired furnishings. The key is to look — it's only a matter of time before you'll see.

Who are you and how do you like to live? What are the recurring themes that can act as the springboard to your decorating scheme? Resolve these questions and you're well on your way to carving out a creative direction that reflects your individual style.

LAYER TWO

Creating your

concept

Your concept

All decorative pursuits, no matter how large or small, should begin with a concept. A concept is an outline of your creative vision; its purpose here is to act as a kind of insurance policy for your interior, guaranteeing that you have flow and cohesion from the front door through to the back. Without an overriding creative concept, your interior falls prey to the possibility of appearing a little higgledy-piggledy. Even if you're planning to decorate in stages, with long intervals between each, it's important to begin the journey with a whole concept. That way, as you decorate each stage or each room, you can refer to your original plans for clarity.

The best way to translate your story into a creative concept is to create a mood board.

Creating a cut-and-paste mood board

Whenever I'm creating a concept — whether it's for a book, a range of products or a decorating scheme — I always play around with a mood board. If you were to witness this process, you might feel that it's a rather childish one. And on the surface of it, it does appear this way. At its core, however, a mood board is one concrete way of transporting the ideas from your mind into the world. Sometimes the ideas are kinda crazy — and when you see them laid out in front of you, this is confirmed — but other times you can really be onto something. A colour might stand out or a general theme may start to emerge, and with this you have your beginning.

The idea behind a mood board is to play around with colour, texture, form, materials and other inspiration, until you find a common thread and balance.

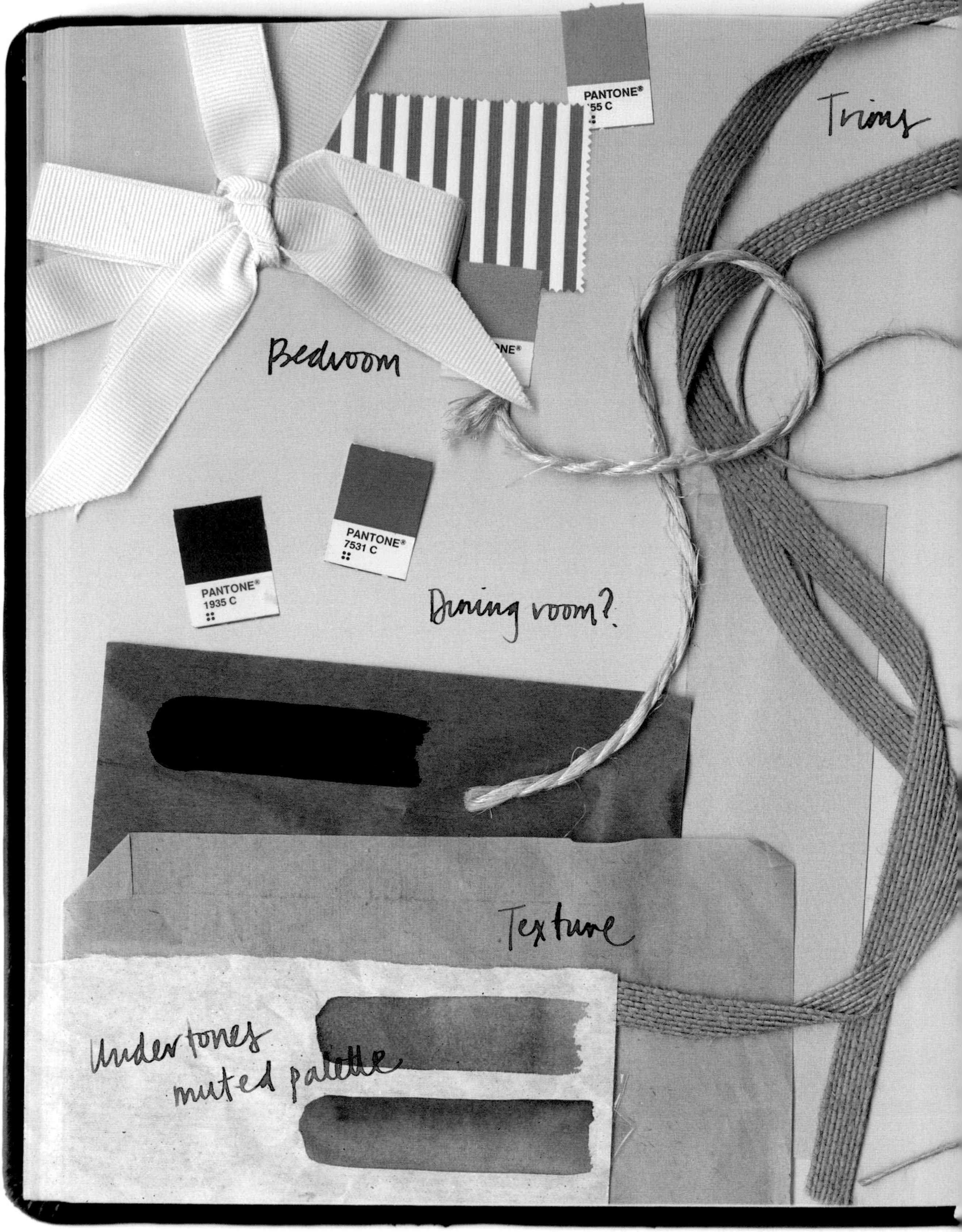

Trims

Bedroom

PANTONE®
'55 C

PANTONE®

PANTONE®
7531 C

PANTONE®
1935 C

Dining room?

Texture

Undertones
muted palette

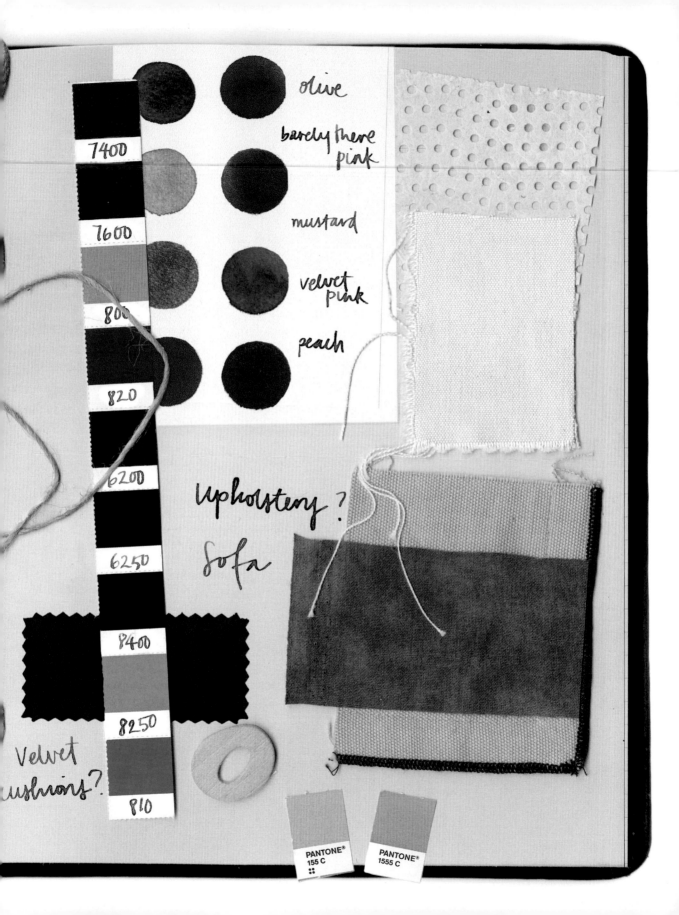

olive

barely there
pink

mustard

velvet
pink

peach

7400

7600

800

820

6200

6250

8400

8250

810

Upholstery?

sofa

Velvet
cushions?

PANTONE®
155 C

PANTONE®
1555 C

You can use anything at all as the backing for your board, from a corkboard to a torn piece of brown paper. Keep moving your inspiration pieces around the board until they're in balance – avoid fastening them down before you're ready.

For your inspiration pieces, collect anything at all that you like: ribbon, cotton, pebbles, stones, magazine clippings, photographs, postcards, stationery, paint and fabric swatches, painted colour brush-outs (see page 88), buttons, cotton reels, jute, twine, leaves, flowers, feathers, shells, tiles, and so on. Keep your scissors handy (or a scalpel, ruler and cutting board) so that you can cut your pieces to a size that feels right for the board. Too much of a bright and geometric fabric swatch might overwhelm your board, for example, so don't be afraid to cut things down to a more manageable size. Interacting with small pieces like this is the precursor to creating a decorating scheme using the real elements. The key is to be playful.

Look at your board critically once you've created the initial layout – and add and take away as required to create a sense of balance. You might find that one colour or texture is outweighing the other elements on the board. This will give you a lead, perhaps inspiring you to use this colour or texture as the base of your interior. Once you've achieved balance and you're completely happy with your mood board, paste or pin everything down.

The virtual mood board

Although I prefer the tangibility of a 'real' mood board, creating a concept on your computer is another great way to see your ideas working together within a framework. You can use any format, from Microsoft Publisher to a PowerPoint presentation or the more advanced Adobe Photoshop or InDesign. Use your scanner to take in images from magazines and any bits and pieces of inspiration you find (you can scan all sorts of things, including ribbon and string) and save them in one easy-to-access folder. Scour the internet for images, graphics, fonts – really, anything that takes your fancy – and save them to the same folder as your scans.

Try not to be too inhibited by a particular colour or style at this stage – the key is to let your imagination run wild. Once you're satisfied with what you've gathered, use your critical eye to decide what will make it to your inspiration page. Move your images around the page until you strike a kind of balance. Layer images over other images; play around with their angles, size, rotation, borders and so on, so that your board develops a kind of depth. Once you're happy, save your board (as a PDF file if you can) and print it out.

Go through this process as many times as you need, until you reach a mood board combination that feels 'just right'.

There are no right or wrong answers when it comes to creating a mood board – you can use either tangible or virtual elements or a mix of the two. The result should unearth the seeds of your creative direction.

From mood board to concept

Once you've created your mood board, it's time to evolve your thoughts to the next stage – into a decorative concept or scheme. Creating a concept requires you to read your mood board with a critical eye, breaking down each piece of inspiration into colours, textures, shape and form. Using these questions as a starting point, write down the dominant themes presented by your board:

COLOUR What's the predominant colour scheme? What tones of colour make up the pictures – bright, muted or pale, for example (see page 81 for more on colour)? What's the background colour, the predominant colour found in most of your inspiration pieces? It may be white or you may have a soft palette of neutrals – ecru, sand and linen, for example, or a soft grey–blue.

What are the over-colours (that is, the main ones) and roughly in what kinds of percentages do they appear? Your board may present a sea theme, for example, with 50 per cent sand colours, 25 per cent blue and 25 per cent green. This is a great indicator of the kind of colour scheme you might use in your own home – it could be you have the walls, floors and major items of furniture in a mix of neutrals and sands, with 25 per cent each of blue and green as the accent colours in your smaller items. If your board includes shiny textures, then these might translate into the fabrics you choose – silks, velvets and metallic linens, for example.

TEXTURE What kinds of textures do you see – shiny, rough, smooth, metallic? Where do the different textures appear – on fabric, flooring or upholstery?

LAYERING How do the colours layer on the board? Are there dominant colours under soft colours or vice versa? Are there block, plain colours at the back and patterns layered over the top?

A mood board is an opportunity to experiment, to play around with colour, texture and form and to balance these elements in a way that creates a sense of harmony. Once you're happy with their relationship, the next step is to evolve your mood board into an actual room scheme. This is where the playing begins to take a more tangible shape, where you can insert actual fabric, patterning and furniture options on your board. And from here, a concept is born!

EXERCISE:

From concept to room scheme

Once you've read your mood board and have begun to work out how your inspiration might translate into a room concept, you'll find that the research process begins again. This time you're on the lookout for things you might actually use in your final decorating scheme.

Creating a clear scheme gives you a solid framework to work within – and a room scheme presented on a board will help you maintain this clarity of vision throughout the process of decorating, which can often be drawn out over many, many months. Follow these steps to create a clear scheme to work from:

1 **SEARCH ONLINE** Using 'Suppliers' on page 200 as a starting point, look for fabrics in the kinds of colours and textures you're after. Make a note of where they're available and order in as many samples as you think you may need (samples are generally free, although with some products you have to pay a small fee). Ditto for tiles, paint colours, and so on. Look for furniture in shapes and styles that suit the look you want to create.

2 **COLLECT IMAGES** Print or cut out any pictures and swatches you feel may fit the bill, then arrange them on a piece of black artist's board in a balanced configuration.

3 **ARRANGE YOUR BOARD** Cut each element to a scale that fits the board (your pieces need to be no larger than a small swatch, about 4 centimetres square). Print out headings and labels using a font that reflects the overall aesthetic and include them. The aim with your board (as with your mood board earlier) is to provide balance on the page; you want your collection to look professional and ordered so as to convey a clear message or 'story'.

4 EXPERIMENT Play around with your ideas, leaving them to rest and then going back to them at intervals, making any adjustments to your choices as you go. Don't be afraid to call in more samples if you feel your palette needs some further tweaking. Sometimes, the process of building a room scheme can be a lengthy one, but the time lapses are also helpful, in that they ensure you're truly happy with your final palette. Your job as a decorator is to edit down the possibilities: don't be tempted to drown the board in every option or sample you've collected. This is decision-making time, so you'll need to choose only one or two samples of each element for the board.

5 KEEP WORKING AT IT If in doubt about your direction, create two or three boards, each with its own well-edited items. Once you're completely happy with the arrangement and balance of your board/s, stick each piece down using double-sided tape.

Collect fabric samples in various colours and patterns; print out furniture and accessory options, and source inspiring rooms and spaces to form the basis of your room scheme. Cut and paste your pieces onto thick black card and voilà, you have developed a solid concept to work to.

LAYER THREE

Working with space

Respect the reality of your space

While developing a vision or concept for your interior is a vital step towards creating a bold and individual home, it's important to marry your ideas with a solid sense of the reality of your space and its limitations. However lofty your plans for your interior, its location, scale and architecture will dictate, to some degree, your creative direction. The process of decorating a home is one of careful editing with a big dollop of compromise thrown in for good measure (unless, of course, you've been fortunate enough to build your home from scratch and entirely to your specifications).

It's best to approach the limitations of your architecture as a kind of joyful challenge, paying it the respect it deserves as you build your creative plans for it. Take note of each room's positive and negative attributes — what you'd like to accentuate and which areas need concealing. Then think clearly about what you need your interior to do for you at this stage of life. While expensive rugs and soft furnishings make for a beautiful space, it will not remain beautiful for long if you have messy toddlers running around with their inevitably dirty hands and feet! And there's little point creating a palace for entertaining at home if your life is too busy with work to even entertain the idea of entertaining.

Creating balance

With each room you're working towards the ideal of balance. In reality, however, unless you're building from scratch, most homes don't come neatly balanced. There are many obstacles to deal with, from odd-shaped rooms to low ceilings, dark spaces, tight fits, and so on. How you approach your decorating can go a long way to rebalancing these little oddities.

The first step is to see the space for what it really is and then marry your decorative response to it. A good way to see a space warts and all is to empty it of all its furniture — its shape and faults will then become very clear. If that's not possible, close your eyes, and visualise the room's framework. Write down its positive and negative attributes, what's working and what isn't. On another page, write down everything you can think of about the room in two columns labelled 'positive' and 'negative'. Once you've determined what's working and what isn't, you can get down to the task of fixing it.

A floor plan for all rooms

There is no one-size-fits-all solution when devising a floor plan — every room has its own advantages, irregularities and quirks — but there's one universal guideline, which is to create a space, regardless of its shape and size, that embodies the ideal of balance and harmony.

The concept of balance and harmony can seem rather esoteric to begin with — it's very subjective and, given that what is balanced in one space won't necessarily be balanced in another, it can be a difficult notion to pin down. The key is to make it tangible, and the best way to do this is to create a floor plan — either a 2D version using good old paper and pencils, or a 3D version using design software such as Google SketchUp. I prefer the paper and pencils option first up, as I like to sketch quickly, mapping out all my options in a free fashion until I reach an arrangement that feels right. Once I have the basic plan in place, I'll turn to my computer for a more precise version, ensuring the plan is in scale and my furniture pieces are in proportion to the walls, windows and each other.

The aim with all spaces, large, small and misshapen, is to create a sense of balance and harmony. Create a floor plan and shuffle around to-scale furniture cut-outs to visualise the ideal layout.

EXERCISE: *Creating a floor plan*

Follow these steps to put together a floor plan for each room:

1 **MEASURE THE SPACE** With notepad and pencil in one hand and builder's tape measure in the other, measure the perimeter of your space, making note of the windows and doors (including frames), light switches, power points and TV antenna connections. Take special note of the ceiling heights plus any picture rails or fireplaces — these measurements will become important a little further down the track.

2 **MEASURE YOUR FURNITURE** Using your builder's tape, measure the length, width and height of all major items of furniture, such as sofa, chairs, coffee and side tables, or beds, making note of their form and detail as you go. If you plan to replace any of the furniture items, make a note of the measurements of the items you intend to buy.

3 **MAKE A BLUEPRINT** Using a pencil and ruler, transfer your findings to a piece of grid paper, maintaining a consistent scale throughout. The ideal scale to work with is 1:20, with 1 centimetre on the grid equal to 20 centimetres in your room. If you're dealing with an extra-large room, you could try 1:50 (1 centimetre on the grid equals 50 centimetres in your room) or even 1:100 (1 centimetre on the grid equals 100 centimetres — one metre — in the room). Play around with various furniture combinations — begin with the largest pieces (such as a sofa or dining table), then work your other furniture around them. Create a number of blueprints, moving your furniture around until you reach a combination that looks and feels most balanced. One fun way to play around with balance is to draw your furniture to scale, cut out the pieces and then shuffle them around your drawn floor plan until you find a configuration that works. You can also play around a bit by trying the styles on page 50.

4 **CREATE EASE OF MOVEMENT** Does your floor plan allow for easy movement around the space? Is there enough room around the dining table for people to sit comfortably? Does the scale of the furniture feel in balance with the scale of the room? Perhaps the furniture is oversized, which can make the space (and you) feel clogged or choked. If the furniture is too small for the room, the space will feel overwhelming, disconnected and uncomfortable — and you'll feel a little like a small fish in a big pond. Work with your plan until it looks just right, remembering that it might take time and a few sketches to come to the best arrangement.

5   **INCORPORATE HOW YOU LIVE IN YOUR SPACE**   Take into account not just the proportions of the furniture and the room, but also how the layout will serve the life you lead at home. A room set up as an open-plan palace of entertainment won't do if you're the private type who likes to cocoon and relax. On the other hand, if you're the gregarious kind who loves natural light, breeze and ease of movement, then a cluttered space with oversized items will become frustrating and downright difficult to live with. Identifying your homely habits and factoring them into your plan will ensure an individualised blueprint and a one-of-a-kind space.

6   **TRUST YOUR GUT FEELING**   While preparing a floor plan and nutting out your placement options on paper or the computer are an important first step, nothing will ensure balance and harmony in a room quite like mucking in and moving your furniture around the space until you reach an ideal arrangement. In the process, you may find that the plan you devised on paper is not the one that comes to life in the room, once the realities of light, airflow and personal connection all come into play. It's at this point that you need to experiment with your options and, most importantly, trust your gut feeling. Listen to how you feel in the room. If the arrangement isn't working for you, then experiment until you find a formation that does.

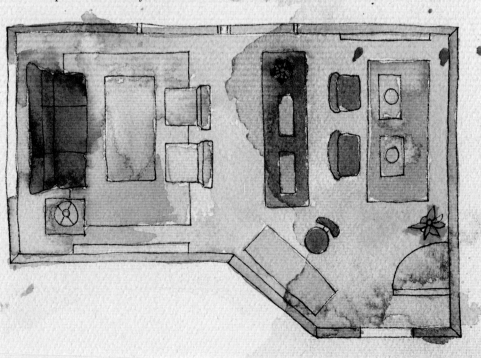

Playing with room styles

When devising your floor plan, the framework of the room will dictate to some degree the best configuration for your furniture pieces. If you have room to play around, however, use these floor-plan styles as a guide to creating exactly the right feeling.

FORMAL   A formal setting evokes a sense of order, using a strict placement of pieces to imbue the room with a certain sense of ceremony. Complete balance is the key here, with nothing on a slant or angle and no 'slouch'. Sofas must be straight and armchairs neatly facing inwards in straight lines!

RELAXED   There's room in a relaxed space for a little disorder — armchairs on an angle, with circular or oval coffee and side tables. The key to a relaxed space is not trying too hard.

OVERSIZED SPACE   These require oversized pieces of furniture, grouped together in vignettes throughout the room. Always avoid placing furniture against the walls, to ensure you don't feel as though you're swimming about.

SMALL SPACE   Avoid a cramped, cluttered space by ensuring your furniture is petite and streamlined, with narrow arms, fine legs and tight upholstery to avoid too much bulk in the room.

GREETING SPACE   Make a feature of the entrance to the room, turning it into a greeting space, by displaying a one-off piece that wows you every time you walk through the door. Avoid clutter at all times in greeting spaces: hatstands, key hooks and general mess should be well and truly hidden elsewhere.

When devising a floor plan, place your larger items of furniture, such as sofa and dining table, into the space first, then the smaller items to fit snugly around them. Be sure there's enough space around each piece for ease of movement and flow.

EXERCISE:

Analyse your favourite space

Think of a space you love spending time in – it could be anything from a friend's house to a restaurant, bar or shop. Loosely sketch the outline of the space on grid paper, including windows and doorways, and then fill in the floor plan with other attributes, such as furniture, lighting, and so on.

Analyse the space and write down its positive and negative traits. What makes this space work so well? How is the furniture placed? What is the relationship between the furniture, the light sources and the doorways and other thoroughfares?

Try the exercise again with another space you love. Once you've tried your hand at what makes other spaces work, then you can apply your skills to your own space, working with its positive and negative attributes and assembling all the elements so that the space can operate as well and as happily as possible.

Having trouble with your floor plan? A good starting point is to analyse a room you love to spend time in, with the aim of unearthing what makes its elements work so well together. Use restaurants, hotel rooms, shops and cafés as your guide, and apply their positive attributes in your own space.

Shaping your backdrop

Choosing your Canvas

While the treatment of your floors and walls is officially in the domain of interior design as they are fixed items (along with the tiles, floorboards, carpets, wall paint and so on) rather than interior decorating, it's important to touch on them here because the plan for your interior might include updating some of these aspects.

I like to think of walls and floors as the canvas in the room – they offer a kind of backdrop and a framework for you to work within. Assessing the framework of your space is an important first step in the process of creative decision-making. The walls and floors should ideally be an extension of the architecture of the home – meaning they should pair seamlessly with your home's style of architecture. Have a look at your space – inside and out. Is it modern, with sharp, clean lines? Or is it industrial perhaps, combining clean-lined architecture with larger, more textured features, such as wide, heavy-set floorboards and exposed plumbing? Or is your home more decorative, with softer lines, such as arches, moulding and ornate cornices, and so more feminine in nature?

Ideally, your choice of wall treatments and flooring should work nicely with your existing architecture. Tough, industrial concrete flooring, for example, is not ideal for an ornate environment. A floorboard treated in a soft tone, such as a white or grey lime wash, offers a more subtle option, allowing ornate decorative elements to shine. On the other hand, a soft and pretty tile could be too gentle for the masculinity of a bold industrial environment. A wide, heavy-set recycled floorboard, bare concrete or a heavy patterned concrete tile would be better suited to this environment. While there are no hard and fast rules, you can use these natural design pairings to guide you and, once you gain decorating confidence, you'll feel freer to push the boundaries.

Walls

Your walls provide a framework for your interior scheme, giving it boundaries, and their decorative treatment provides a backdrop to your space. The choices you make for your walls are integral – as they set the tone for the rest of your scheme. But which direction should you go: whitewashed, coloured, textured, or swathed in wallpaper? There are many questions to ask yourself before you make your final choices; make sure you get out your pad and pencil and write down some answers.

Wallpaper

I love wallpaper, and have felt particularly inspired in recent years, as there are so many interesting styles, designs and colours to choose from, whether richly coloured and patterned or simple and contemporary. For me, wallpaper is a form of art (imagine the hours, days and weeks that have gone into the creation of a single paper) – it's a way of bringing the bricks and mortar to life and softening a home's architecture.

At its best, a room or a single wall covered in wallpaper will add another dimension to your interior scheme. It will stamp your space with character and – most exciting – individualise your interior. Choosing from the enormous selection of patterns, palettes and backing papers available can be rather an overwhelming task. As is always the case with interior decorating, success lies in how you whittle down the options. Use this step-by-step plan to find a paper that fits your style and your room:

1   **ARCHITECTURE**   Use the architecture of your home as the starting point for your style direction. If your space is contemporary – with clean lines and no elaborate detailing (such as ceiling cornices and decorative skirting boards) – then reflect this simplicity in your wallpaper. If your home is more decorative, with an old-world flavour, then a more intricately patterned paper (such as one by Florence Broadhurst or Osborne & Little) will fit the bill.

2   **GENRE**   The wallpaper you choose needs to complement the genre (or function) of the room as well as provide beautiful decoration. For a playroom, for example, which needs to evoke life and spirit, a high-energy pattern in an upbeat palette of red or aqua is ideal. For a bedroom, which should be infused with tranquillity and peace, a simple pattern in a nature-inspired palette is perfect.

Ah, wallpaper, wallpaper. Could there be anything more beautiful than walls lined with the stuff? If you choose your wallpaper with love in mind, and the understanding that it's artwork in its own right, it will become the focus in a room. Furnish around it accordingly.

3   **VOICE**   It might sound rather crazy to think of your walls as a person, but there is method to the madness! Seeing your walls as a person with a voice and a tale to tell will help you refine the kind of energy and ambience you're hoping to achieve with your wallpaper selection. What would you like your walls to be saying to you? If it's, 'I'm a laid-back, carefree and relaxed kind of space that enjoys light and sunshine', a simple pattern in a soft and pale palette (think blues and greens) is the direction for you. If your walls are dramatic and stately, the kind that love rich, layered patterns in a sophisticated palette of gold, greens, reds and purples, then begin your journey with wallpaper designers that reflect this aesthetic (see 'Suppliers' on page 200).

4   **SCHEME**   Colour is everything and your colour palette will bring your wallpaper pattern to life. Look to the colour section on page 81 to hone your colour palette. If you're a novice decorator, stick to the palette you've created, but if you're a confident decorator and want to create a mixed and eclectic room scheme, you can play around with colour in your wallpaper choices. Just be sure that the colours you do choose are of the same weight – or the same tone – as your palette, to avoid the room feeling overly busy.

5   **EDIT**   Heading out to the wallpaper showroom or trawling internet sites and wading through the thousands of options available can be an overwhelming task. Be sure to write your plan of attack before you leave the house or go online, as, like a kid in a candy store, it's easy to go astray. Begin with the architecture, style or genre you're working with – traditional, modern, children's – and then the voice you're trying to echo. Keep your style guide handy, to avoid being tempted by all the other options, but don't be afraid to fall in love with a paper that wasn't necessarily on your agenda – sometimes it's the ones we least expected to find that make our hearts sing the loudest. Don't be afraid to ask for samples to take home with you – if they don't have the sample you're after, they'll be happy to mail it to you later.

6   **EXPERIMENT**   Don't be too hasty in making a decision – wallpaper is pretty permanent, so you need to make your choice with certainty and insight. Tape your samples to the wall and live with them for a week or even a month to ensure that the love affair wasn't a fleeting one and you're in for the long haul. Once you're sure, however, take the leap without wasting a minute, as there's nothing more exciting than turning a wallpaper dream into a design reality.

7   **MIX AND MATCH**   It's possible to mix and match wallpapers, both in different rooms in the one house, and on different walls in the same room. The key to assuring continuity throughout the space is to work within the same genre (contemporary, chintz, classic floral) or in the same colour palette and colour weighting. A contemporary wallpaper with a simple pattern does not pair well with an intricate chintz, for example.

8   **APPLY**   There's no one way to apply wallpaper – you can put it on all the walls in a room or just one, on furniture, in cupboards, behind beds. If you're after a cocooning, fully decorated look, choose to swathe all four walls in paper, but be sure to keep the rest of your furnishings simple, as the wallpaper will be the main aesthetic element. Papering one wall as a feature (perhaps behind the bed or sofa or in an entrance) will add a decorative element without overwhelming the space, allowing you to introduce decoration in other ways. Bear in mind that split and half walls won't do the wallpaper justice (and will also make it trickier to apply).

There are many ways to incorporate wallpaper without putting it on your walls. Wallpaper hidden inside your linen cupboard doors adds an element of surprise and a flash of colour. Wallpaper on your pantry shelves or inside cutlery drawers is a quiet way of utilising colour and pattern without them overwhelming the whole room.

Paint

When decorating, it's important to build a happy relationship with paint, as it's a major component in any interior scheme. Out of all of the questions I've been asked about decorating over the years, how to use paint and which colours to choose are at the top of the list. I think the fear lies in the fact that paint is such a permanent proposition. It can be costly, too, and your paint choices can influence every other creative decision you make – so you want to get it right. To help you with your choices, ask yourself these questions and follow these steps:

1 **COLOUR ROLE**   Are your walls a backdrop or a main player in your interior scheme? If they're a backdrop, then head for a neutral, white or subdued tone. This way, the walls will play a supporting role to the furnishings and upholstery. If, on the other hand, the walls are a main player, then you can afford to add lift and colour.

2 **COLOUR TONE**   What style are you hoping to generate in the space: cosy, bright, coastal, country? Pure tones will lift the space, making it bright and breezy; muted tones are ideal for wintry country settings; neutrals in anything from off-white to beige and sand make for a serene, beachy style; electric brights will keep you on your toes and are ideal for high-energy spaces such as offices and kids' playrooms; and pastels are soft and barely there – think pinks for babies' rooms and lavenders for powder rooms. Once you've settled on a tone, you're one step closer to editing down the colour cards on offer.

3 **COLOUR MOOD**   Use what you discovered when creating your decorating story (see page 15) to come up with a basic scheme. Then refer to the 'Colour Personalities' section (see page 91) and ensure that you're happy to live with the colour of your choice. There's nothing worse than choosing a red only to discover that its high-energy, over-the-top nature is driving you a little nuts! If you love the energy of red, but need to tone it down a little, choose a more muted tone. Perhaps blue was an option, but your family is already sleepy enough without its soothing, calm nature. In this case a colour with a little more kick – such as yellow or a more energetic cobalt blue – could be more your scene. Experiment until you settle on a colour that ticks all the boxes.

4 **COLOUR CHARTS**   Armed with a colour direction, head to the paint shop and spend some time perusing the colour charts. Take your time: there's no rush – colouring is an important step and you should be patient. You may need to make a few trips to the paint shop before you

A deep, dark colour on the walls – such as chocolate, charcoal or steely blue – anchors a space, giving a room a solid framework and root system. Lighter, more whimsical tones – such as pale, pale grey, blue and off-white – elevate a space, lifting the spirit and energy of a room.

feel like you've looked at everything on offer. Once you're focused, choose some colour chips – as many as you like (they're free!) – to take home with you. Add them to your mood board or colour scheme and let them sit for a while before you make any judgements. Then begin to edit the choices until you've narrowed the field to a few options. Another option is to invest in a fan deck from your favourite paint supplier (which includes every colour, texture and finish they have available), as it will become a worthwhile resource when you're in the throes of creating your room schemes. All paint companies, large or small, offer these for purchase, either as large folders, or streamlined, easy-to-manage booklets. Invest in as many as you can, as the more you get into decorating the more you'll find you need to refer to them.

5   **COLOUR SAMPLES**   Now that you have a few colour options in mind, buy some sample pots and use them to create some brush-outs (see page 88 for more). Apply the colour directly to the wall in question or to a piece of white or off-white butcher's paper then use masking tape to stick the paper to the wall. (Avoid brushing out dark colours directly on the wall, as they're too hard to cover up again.) To get a true sense of how your colour choice works, your sample should be at least 1 ×× 1 metre. You should also apply it to either end of your room, as the colour could change from one end of the room to the other, depending on how the light affects the space. Live with your brush-outs on the wall for at least a week, making note of how they change and evolve over time.

6   **COLOUR CHOICE**   Take the plunge! If you've done the research, applied your samples to the wall and lived with them for a while, then it's time to take the colour leap: invest in your paint colour and paint, paint, paint. Don't be afraid of getting it wrong – even the most experienced decorator makes a mistake or two at times. Begin with one wall and assess how it works. You'll know if it's the right one – your gut will tell you so! If you're still unsure, have faith and confidence in the process you've been through to make it this far, but don't be afraid to go back to the drawing board if need be.

Developing a relationship with paint requires constant attention – you must engage with paint regularly to be confident using it. To see how paint will look and feel in a room, invest in sample pots, create brush-outs on off-white or white butcher's paper, then pin them to the wall. Experimentation is the key.

Paint finishes and textures

The paint finish and texture you choose for your home will add another dimension to the feeling and visual effect you're going for. All paint companies offer their own names and variations on the finishes I've outlined below. Before you make any specific purchase, speak at length with your local paint supplier so you know exactly what you're buying and that the product is appropriate for the task. The usual options are:

MATT OR FLAT   This modern and slightly textured paint, which offers little in the way of gloss or shine, works just as well on bricks or concrete as on flat Gyprock. It creates a relaxed backdrop and is ideal for bright sunny spaces (as the textured nature of the paint softens the glare). Avoid it if you have little ones with dirty fingers — matt paint is very tricky to clean.

SATIN OR SEMI-GLOSS   A step up from matt in terms of shine and shimmer, satin or semi-gloss paints are smoother in texture, look and feel. They're ideal for walls of all kinds, as they're simple to apply and very easy to keep clean and fresh — a must if you want to combine white walls with toddlers.

GLOSS   The shiniest of them all, gloss paint possesses a shimmery texture that cannot be ignored. Gloss paint is ideal for doorways and trims, such as skirting boards and mantels, as the glossier finish offsets matt or satin walls beautifully. Remember, though, that gloss paint dulls after a time, and the initial super-glossy finish will eventually soften back to a subtle gloss.

TEXTURED OR CEMENT   With fine particles of texture (often sand) included, cement or textured paints add a rough and grainy finish to an otherwise smooth surface. They're perfect over brick and block walls, as they add another textural dimension. It's best to avoid this finish on timber, however.

METALLIC   Add glimmer and a little 'bling' to your walls by using a metallic paint finish. Metallic paints come in a range of colours — from mauve to blue, green, white and silver. Their shimmery nature adds another dimension to the space, and the softer colour palettes make them a subtle feature in a room.

The paint finish you choose — matt, gloss or textured — will greatly affect your colour choice and the mood in a room. It's a good idea to sample your colour in the finish you want, to ensure the outcome is exactly as you hoped.

What paint where?

Paint does more than just infuse a space with colour, it's also an effective way to highlight the positive aspects of a room while concealing its negatives. Try these tricks to overcome any shortcomings in a space:

LOW CEILING   Painting a low ceiling white (or a very light colour) will create the illusion of height in the room.

HIGH CEILING   A high ceiling can benefit from a deeper colour. Stick with a neutral if you're after a simple backdrop, or wrap the room in a colour to make a statement. For a cosier feel, avoid white on the ceilings – perhaps a grey or light taupe is a better option.

DARK SPACE   It's a common response to paint a dark room in a light colour (often white), as the colour will reflect much-needed light into the space. But avoid this option if your space is not only dark but also cold. Instead, add warmth by using a golden tone, or take it one step further and use a deep, dark colour on the walls to create a boudoir-like aesthetic. Stick to a light but warm colour on the ceiling to avoid the space becoming too oppressive.

LIGHT SPACE   Avoid wrapping the walls in a bright white paint, which will only add to the glare. Go instead for an off-white infused with a touch of yellow or warm grey. If the space is light and hot, choose a cooling tone, such as an icy grey, blue or green. Add a slightly deeper tone to the ceiling to counterbalance the extra glare.

OVERSIZED SPACE   Create cosiness in an oversized room by opting for a deep, muted colour. This is the ideal environment to play around with texture, too – a metallic or roughly textured paint (for more, see 'Paint Finishes and Textures' on page 67) will add an interesting dimension.

SMALL ROOM   Create the illusion of space by opting for a pale, pure tone from any end of the spectrum, based on the kind of colour personality (see page 91) you can live with. If the room is not only small but also lacking sunlight and a little bit cold, then move to a warmer tone – still pale, but with a little touch of yellow as the undertone. White on the ceiling will give the room a feeling of height.

MOULDINGS, CORNICES, DOORS, SKIRTING BOARDS   If your ceiling is white, then stick with white mouldings and cornices. Skirting boards and doors are also ideally suited to white, but can be painted in a darker or lighter tone of the colour you're using on the walls.

Be creative in the way you apply your paint colour to the walls – paint your door in stripes, in two tones of the same colour; paint your door frames and rails in an accent colour; or go for a bold, bright colour on a feature wall.

Paint formulations

Which paint formulation you choose has more to do with how easy it is to use and clean up than with the final look of your space.

ACRYLIC   Water-based acrylic paints are easy to apply and easy to clean up. Their formula is more flexible than that of enamel paints, so they're easier to manage and they give better coverage with both brush and roller. Better still, acrylic paints are considered more eco-friendly, as they don't require toxic thinners or turpentine.

ENAMEL   Available only in semi-gloss and gloss formulas, oil-based enamels are hard-drying and have traditionally been preferred for timber trims such as doors, door frames and skirtings because of their hard-wearing nature. The downside is that oil-based enamels yellow over time, so your whites will become cream, particularly in direct sunlight. Enamels are also tricky to clean up, requiring copious amounts of turpentine. Acrylic paints have taken over recently because they're easier to use and clean up.

LIME WASH   On both interior and exterior walls a lime wash lends a lovely soft and mottled effect, giving an aged impression to the surface – the kind you find on the old-world villas of Tuscany and Provence. A lime-washed surface will not have a flat, uniform finish and will emphasise any irregularities, but this just adds to the effect. As traditional lime washes are free of petrochemicals, they're ideal for the environmentally minded decorator. To achieve the best mottled effect, apply by brush in random directions, maintaining a wet edge throughout the application process to prevent wet–dry overlaps. Two coats are required to achieve the best depth of colour and finish.

CEMENT   Ideal for exposed cement-block, rendered or brick surfaces, cement paint is hard-wearing, textural and resilient. Cement paints are available in a matt finish only, their colours drying to a soft, aged-looking patina. These paints are a great option for covering up 1970s brickwork without the expense of bagging or rendering. For a uniform finish, apply the paint with a wide brush and ensure all nooks and crannies are filled.

WOOD WASH   With a translucent formula that shows the wood grain and adds a textural dimension, wood wash lends a soft and velvety look and feel to natural wood. The water-based formula makes wood wash very low in toxicity and odour. It's a lovely paint finish to use, particularly if you're after a Nordic feel.

Pressed metal applied to the wall before painting can add some texture to walls and ceilings in a subtle and beautiful way. It comes in numerous designs, from dainty floral prints to grand art deco patterning, so there's an option to suit every style of home.

Floors

The role of the floors in your space is literally to ground the decorative scheme, providing a metaphorical 'root system' for all the other elements that make up a room. The colour and type of floor covering you choose will go a long way towards defining how you want to feel in the space. Just like the walls, your floors act as a backdrop to your entire decorating scheme, so it's important to choose their material and tone wisely. The basic options are:

HARDWOOD TIMBER   If your floors are the 'root system' then timber flooring is the most natural choice. Timber makes an ideal backdrop to almost every decorative scheme. Timber floorboards lend a linear aesthetic, providing a link from one part of the house to the next. They work in all rooms of the house (even the bathroom when mixed with a tile in the wet areas). Some are stained (for example deep chocolate or grey–ash) to give them a deeper, more uniform finish. Most are finished in satin or gloss polyurethane to ensure longevity and give the floor a soft sheen. A more natural finish is oil or wax, but this needs to be redone frequently.

LAMINATE FLOORBOARDS   This synthetic product, which aims to simulate natural timber floorboards, consists mostly of melamine board coated with a thin layer of laminate. Laid in a gridlock system then glued in place, laminate floorboards are hardwearing. They're a much cheaper option if your budget won't stretch to hardwood flooring, but will never replace its look, feel and character.

CARPET   Cosy and comfortable carpet has been enjoying a renaissance of late in the world of design. Wool is the most natural and warmest of the carpet types – being a pure fibre, it's soft, it breathes and it has low emissions. There are many piles on offer – from plush to loop and twist, self-patterned, subtly flecked, in a flat colour or busily patterned. There are also several types of carpet fibre on offer: wool, wool with nylon, nylon, sisal, coir. If your carpet is only a backdrop, stick with a plush pile in a uniform colour. If it's a player in your scheme, you can go for one infused with some interest. Remember, however, that any pattern or colour fleck becomes part of your scheme – and so you'll need to organise your other furnishings to accommodate this extra element. Get a sample before you order and lay your carpet, so that you can play with it until it works in your room scheme. (See also 'Floor Rugs' on page 182.)

Your floors will form the backdrop to your whole interior scheme and so it's important to consider their texture, form and colour when building your decorating concept. Base your flooring choices on how you'd like to feel in your space.

Tiles

Tiles create a durable and long-lasting floor finish that's easy to clean and maintain. They're ideal if you're living in a warm climate, as they'll keep your space cool (while underfloor heating will keep it warm in winter). There are several different types of tile available, each with its own unique attributes:

CERAMIC   Ceramic tiles are made of clay and are available in either glazed or unglazed varieties. Go for unglazed on the floor in wet areas to avoid slips.

PORCELAIN   These ceramic tiles are extremely hardwearing and offer very low porosity. They're ideal for wet areas such as the laundry and bathroom. Go for glazed tiles on the walls in these places, and stick with unglazed on the floors.

TERRACOTTA   Literally 'baked earth', terracotta is a warm and natural material for floors as it mimics the earth beneath our feet. The colour of the tile will largely depend on where it's sourced – Italian terracotta often has more of an orange tinge, whereas Portuguese terracotta will be slightly pink. Terracotta is a highly porous material and will require diligent sealing to prevent staining.

GLASS MOSAICS   Offered in an extensive range of colours and patterns, glass mosaic tiles are hardwearing and provide a beautifully decorative finish. They're best suited to low-traffic, smaller spaces – such as bathroom floors and walls, and kitchen splashbacks – as the large amounts of grout can be difficult to keep clean, particularly if you choose a white grout.

STONE   Being a natural material, stone tiles such as marble and granite provide a beautiful feel underfoot. Some stones are harder than others – the most porous of them require regular sealing to prevent staining.

CONCRETE   A popular choice, particularly for modern industrial environments, concrete flooring is hardwearing, easy to clean and aesthetically interesting. The concrete is ground to create a smooth surface and then honed to produce a buffed, smooth finish. Adding a pigment to the concrete produces a coloured slab. If the slab is already in situ, a pigmented 40 millimetre topping can be laid over it before polishing.

Patterned tiles on a floor offer colour and artistic form, so it's important to regard them as part of your overall decorating scheme. In a space that otherwise employs solids in neutral tones, a patterned floor tile will become a most sophisticated focus.

ANTIQUE AND REPRODUCTION TILES These one-of-a-kind tiles, with their unique pattern and colour possibilities, provide a layer of interest and individuality in a way that standard block-colour tiles just can't. If you're lucky enough to have antique tiles (often salvaged from old-world homes in France and Argentina), they'll immediately infuse your space with depth and soul. But if sourcing great antique tiles is not an option, a multitude of reproduction tiles is available for a fraction of the price. These tiles are generally made with a thicker profile than modern tiles, so be sure to have a sample handy if you're pairing them with standard tiles.

Tiles need to be coated with a sealant specifically formulated for that tile. Always check with your tile supplier before you purchase, to ensure you know the best option for the job at hand.

LAYER FIVE

Becoming friends
with colour

Colour — there's nowhere to hide

Take a look at any interior scheme and you'll notice that colour appears in every nook and cranny – from the colour of the floorboards beneath your feet to the tones in a patterned cushion, bedspread, light fitting or carpet. Every aspect of interior decorating requires a thorough understanding of colour – our relationship with it, the relationships between different colours and how each colour relates to our environment. Colour is a layered – and overwhelming – subject. Just when you think you have the knack of it, it goes and changes on you, reinventing itself at any opportunity.

A successful interior, one that hangs together with a strong thread and a solid sense of self, hinges on how you utilise colour in your space. Employing colour with confidence requires a commitment of sorts – to dive into a relationship with it, to unravel all of its layers, to infiltrate its nuances and to get wholly inside it. It sounds exhausting and, in part, engaging with colour in this way is a draining process. Many a decorator has been known to avoid the subject, preferring to stick to an entirely neutral palette.

Being a colour junkie myself, I say that any time you put into your relationship with colour will be worth it in the end. Infusing your interior scheme with colour will bring the space to life, giving it energy, verve and personality in a way no other aspect of decorating can. The process of tackling colour requires a certain degree of risk-taking – you must make a creative leap at some stage and plunge into it. Practice is the only way to become a deft hand at colour, and once you begin, you'll find that colour really isn't scary at all.

It's important to go through the entire process detailed here, before you begin making any colour choices for your interior. It's the only way to be sure you have a true grasp of this wild and woolly subject. Throw yourself into the theory of colour – every great master had to learn the subject from the ground up before they overstepped the boundaries.

Regard colour as an ongoing education. Our view of it can change depending on our stage of life, our environment, our emotional state, our circumstances, and so on. You'll need to fine-tune your skills from time to time, and with that more deeply penetrate the subject. This section is a colour taster – it will give you a basic understanding of colour, enough to begin your own journey. With that in mind, it's a good idea to read widely – both theoretical books on colour and books on the masters of colour, such as Gauguin, Monet and Van Gogh. Studying their unique approaches will give you a broader understanding of colour and its varying interpretations and applications.

More than any other element, colour brings a room to life, so it's important to feel comfortable using it. Once you get the knack of it, you'll find that experimenting with colour is one of the most exciting and rewarding decorating elements of all.

Colour wheel 101

The colour wheel is a system that has been created specifically to help us understand colours and their relationships to one another. It's a visual representation of primary, secondary, tertiary and complementary colours.

Although it's important to recognise the positive attributes of the colour wheel when you begin your design journey, once you understand it, feel free to break the 'rules'. I do believe that the best in creativity stems from a freer, more experimental and less theoretical approach to colour.

Reading the colour wheel

PRIMARY COLOURS   Red, blue and yellow sit at the centre of the colour wheel.

SECONDARY COLOURS   Formed by mixing two primary colours, giving orange (yellow and red), purple (red and blue) and green (blue and yellow).

TERTIARY COLOURS   Made by mixing one primary colour with one secondary colour, for example yellow plus orange, green plus blue, red plus purple.

COMPLEMENTARY COLOURS   Colours that sit opposite each other on the colour wheel work well together – for example, yellow and purple, red and green or orange and blue. An easy and effective way to use colour in an interior, particularly if you're a novice, is to choose complementary colours in a range of tones from their palest to their darkest. This will ensure that your colour scheme is pleasing to the eye.

CHROMA   This is the intensity, purity or saturation of a colour, and indicates how much white, grey or black it contains. The brighter a colour, the more saturated it is.

VALUE   This indicates whether a colour is light or dark – pale pink is low in value, for example.

TINT   A tint of a colour is created when white is added to that colour. This is usually expressed as a percentage of the colour.

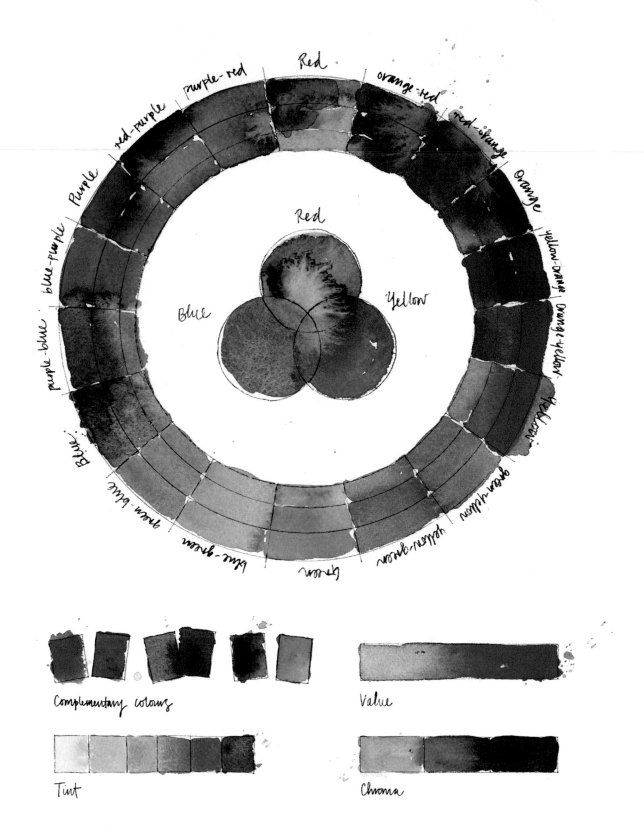

Red

purple-red

red-purple

Purple

blue-purple

purple-blue

Blue

green-blue

blue-green

Green

yellow-green

green-yellow

Yellow

orange-yellow

yellow-orange

Orange

red-orange

orange-red

Red

Blue

Yellow

Complementary colours

Value

Tint

Chroma

The whole world is a colour wheel

Take a second to look around you with an analytical eye – you'll see that every colour you can think of is out there on the most imaginative and interactive mood board there is: the world around us. Sure, it's broad and a little overwhelming for me to say, 'Just turn to the world as your guide,' but if you do take on the challenge you'll be forever rewarded, I promise. Nature offers us every possible colour nuance, over which we can add our built environment, and our personal interpretation of colour.

If you really want to wrangle the world of colour, get yourself out of the house and into the world. Look. See. Break down what you see into bite-sized pieces. Always carry a camera with you and snap anything and everything that you see and love. Download your photos into a folder called something like 'My World'. Break them down into smaller folders for each colour if it helps. Then choose your favourites and start colour matching. Using a standard colour system – a paint fan deck, Pantone book, Color-aid papers or any other system you like – give a name to the colours in your pictures. You might find that one picture contains a palette of five, ten or even twenty colours. Cut and paste the swatches of those colours onto a single piece of paper, along with a printout of the original photo. Then refine the colour scheme to no more than five of your favourites – and voilà, you have a palette from which to begin your overall decorating scheme. After a time and as you gain colour confidence, you might merge the colours from two favourite pictures, taking a special tone from one and adding it to another.

Colour apps

The wonderful thing about technology is that it really does make life so much easier – including the world of creativity and design. Always be on the lookout for mobile phone apps that will help you interpret the world around you within a manageable colour system. Many paint companies have created their own apps – just point and shoot your phone at a particular object or scene, and with the click of a button you can convert the scene into a paint colour palette. What a quick and easy way to match your inspiration to a virtual fan deck!

Have a good look around you and see the world in all its colour glory. Look at how colours interact with each other. What tones of colour work best together as the ideal backdrop hues? What makes some colours 'pop' and in what percentages do they appear? Take photographs to record your findings or, if you're the painterly type, pen or paint your favourite tones and combinations in a workbook.

EXERCISE: Brushing out colours

This exercise is a must for anyone who's attempting to understand colour on a deeper level. Brushing out colours is used to teach art and design students how mixing colours can make another colour and how different amounts of paint can alter the colour outcome. It's an experimental exercise, and since the more you play around with and mix different colours, the more varied your results will be, it needs to be done repeatedly if you really want to develop a relationship with colour.

You'll need plain, unlined index card from a stationer's store and paints, preferably gouache, which has a lovely texture to work with, or acrylic. Avoid oil paint, as it's more difficult to manipulate, particularly if you're a novice. For this exercise it's best to stick to the basic paint colours, such as alizarin crimson, cadmium orange, cadmium yellow, lemon yellow, thalo green, thalo blue, ultramarine blue, violet, titanium white and black. You'll also need two or three paintbrushes, a mixing palette (you can improvise here) and a small bowl of water for cleaning your brushes. The most important elements you'll need, however, are your sense of fun and adventure and a good chunk of time.

Begin by mixing two of your primary colours – say alizarin crimson and cadmium yellow – to create a third colour, then apply this colour to one end of one index card and make notes about the colour proportions on the card. Now, vary the amount of one colour – add more cadmium yellow, for example – and apply the result to another index card. Continue to add a little more of that colour (brushing each result onto an index card as you go), making sure that you step your colours up in small increments. Once you've explored this combination, then go back to the beginning and add more of the second colour – alizarin crimson – to the mix, again working in very small increments and applying each result to the end of an index card.

Practise this with various colour combinations, noting the changes in colour as you go and indexing how you made those changes. The more brush-outs you do, the more you'll build your relationship with colour, and the more you'll understand the effect that one colour can have on another.

Also look at the colour tab on your favourite computer program and no doubt you'll be presented with a slider that takes your chosen colour from light to dark, and transparent to opaque.

Begin with a colour in its most basic form and use the colour slider to take that colour up and down the intensity scale. Add a dash of yellow to the shade, or a touch more blue or red, and you'll change the nature of the colour again. Soon you'll be able to visualise the scale in your mind.

Colour personalities

I like to think about colour in terms of its character traits, the little things that make each colour real, the good points and the not-so-great points, the little idiosyncrasies that make a particular colour interesting. I find this approach humanises the subject and makes it a little easier to decide whether or not you can live with the positive and negative attributes of a particular colour. Although colour appears to be a passive decorative element in a room, it really acts as if it's a living organism.

Each colour we lay our eyes on inspires a physiological and emotional reaction in us, even if we're unaware of it much of the time. Before you invite a particular colour into your space for a lengthy stay, it's important to know exactly who you'll be living with. Although it's fair to say that colour affects each of us differently, there are some universal guidelines to help us navigate this vast subject.

As is always my advice, stick within the guidelines as you build your decorating confidence, but once you feel confident, play around, push the boundaries and even turn the colour theories on their head. Colour is subjective, after all, and how you feel about it can change completely from one stage of your life to another. The key to getting along with colour is to engage with it and all its crazy nuances. The effort will be worth it. You'll see.

Red

The agitator of the spectrum, red is exciting, full of energy and switched on 24/7. At its purest, it's an intense colour with relentless confidence, one that says 'notice me' at every glance. Red affects us deeply on a physiological level – our heartbeat increases at a mere glimpse. Yes, red does raise your metabolism. It gets you going. It gives you a kick.

It goes without saying, then, that red can be a difficult colour to live with full-time. It's like having a hyperactive child in the room (all the time) and so you need a certain degree of bravery to take it on. On the flipside, while red can be exhausting for some, it's highly exhilarating for others. If you're the retiring, laid-back type, red can be just the tonic, giving you a burst of enthusiasm, a lust for life and an energy boost. If you love red but can only live with a dollop, then apply it in small amounts in soft furnishings rather than swathe a whole wall in it. Take some of the heat out of red and you have a lovely nurturing colour that offers energy without tipping you over the edge.

Red, red – you crazy partygoer! There's no rest for the wicked when red's about. Red adds life, vibrancy and verve to any space, particularly the purist and brightest reds in the pack. Ask yourself if you can live with this relentlessly excitable colour.

Yellow

At its best yellow is happy, upbeat, bright and full of beans. It offers a constant diet of intense joy, and everyone who basks in its sunshine is warmer and happier for it. The flipside to all this joy, however, is that yellow can be relentlessly in your face and downright annoying. Yellow can be rather saccharine, and needs to be mixed with a robust colour palette to ensure the space has depth and interest. On the other hand, yellow is ideal for rounding out an already intense and heavy interior — in a room filled with a muted palette of greys and aubergines, for example, it can add a light-hearted breath of fresh air or touch of frivolity. Take yellow down the scale a little — say, to a soft wattle or further to a muted wheat — and you have a very agreeable colour indeed, one that gives a space happy energy but doesn't leave you feeling perpetually irritated.

Orange

Rarely these days do you see orange gracing an interior in all its bright and optimistic glory. Not since the late 1960s and 1970s, when orange was ubiquitous (as part of a palette with brown and yellow), has this joyful colour had its turn on the interior-design stage. Now relegated to the back blocks and the supermarket shelves (think suntan lotion and breakfast cereal), orange has really had its turn out in the cold. It's a shame, though, because it's such an optimistic and hopeful colour. Orange inspires warmth, creativity, fun and the desire to dig deep into the heart and soul. When orange is around, we feel more expressive, more able to engage with our inner self and set it free. Orange inspires us to connect with our instincts, putting us in touch with our true nature. Why wouldn't we want a little orange around?

Could it be that all that happiness is simply too much for us to live with? Well, take it down to the soft and pure end of the scale and you've got yourself a gentle apricot tone with possibly a touch of pinky salmon, which must be due for a renaissance. Make it a muted earthy orange and you're in for a colour that's both deep and divine, ideal when mixed with a Moroccan or Tuscan palette of warm reds, chocolate browns and olive greens.

Yellow's a chirpy colour — happy, upbeat and ever so cheery — but the flipside is that it can be a little too happily 'in your face'. A dollop here and there will prevent you feeling irritated by it.

Green

Oh green, green — your mere presence inspires us to exhale, to decompress, to relax. Anyone who knows me well knows that I've been having a love affair with green for a while now. As a 1970s baby, I spent my formative years living with a palette dominated by red and orange. In those young, carefree days I could cope with such a racy palette — I loved being surrounded by its fiery and passionate nature. That all changed when I hit my thirties, got married, bought my first house, had two children and walked the ever-precarious tightrope between being a mother, a wife and a working woman. Red was just too much to bear, too energetic, too hyperactive, too confrontational. Green became its replacement and I haven't looked back.

Green is the loveliest of colours to live with when life becomes complicated and we need our interiors to offer us a reprieve. Green, calming and gentle, a giver of life, offers us a place to breathe.

Blue

Blue, calming and peaceful, ethereal, mystical and all-knowing, offers us a connection to the heavenly skies above and the deep ocean below. Blue, the colour of confidence, is simultaneously self-possessed and modest. Its effect is all-encompassing, supporting us in a gentle embrace. Living with blue is like living with a kind of peace — it evokes a deep sense of calm and of self. It's no wonder then that blue is so popular among decorators — who could ignore its tranquil allure? If your life could do with an infusion of calm, blue might be just what you need.

A particular tone of blue will imbue your space with a unique feeling. A pure and transparent wash of aqua will evoke the relaxation of whiling away the hours on a tropical island. A brighter cobalt blue (which contains a large dollop of energetic red), while zingy and full of life, will simultaneously evoke serenity and vitality. A steely grey–blue, the kind you might find on a wild and wintry English coastline, takes on some of the attributes of grey — it's chilly, even a little icy and slightly disconnected. A soft pastel blue is pure peace.

'Blue and green should never be seen' — or so they used to say in days long gone. For me, there's no lovelier combination. Stick to the softer versions to avoid clashes, and you have a very agreeable combination of colours indeed.

Brown

If you need more solid ground in your life, then brown in all its tones, from light beige to deep chocolate, is exactly the colour you should invite in. Brown is the colour of the earth beneath our feet, the very thing that upholds life. Brown will have the same supportive effect in your interior as it does in nature. Floor coverings in this palette make an ideal base upon which to layer a plethora of other tones. In fact, most other colours in the spectrum pair beautifully with brown. Brown is best playing the supporting role in an interior, and all other colours will shine against it. A palette only of browns is an overbearing housemate, offering little in the way of lightheartedness and fun, but pair it with blue, green, pink, orange or yellow and you have the ideal balance of strength and excitement.

PANTONE®
473

PANTONE®
1535 U

Pink

Pink's soft, loving nature embraces all who cross its path. Step into a room adorned with pink (particularly at the softer end of the pink scale) and prepare yourself to be soothed by its gentle sweetness. Babies' rooms are the most traditional and obvious spaces for pink, but infusing your living areas, en suite bathrooms, even your office with a touch of pink will bring a sense of peace to those spaces.

Blending pink with a broader palette (of, say, yellows, browns and greens) takes some of the femininity from the tone, and allows it to be employed for the whole family. Use a warm, muted pink in your palette for a sophisticated take on the tone. Go for a bright pink if you prefer the livelier aspects of the red end of the scale. This can also help lift an otherwise struggling interior.

PANTONE®
198 U

Purple

There's a higher-mindedness to purple – it's the hue most associated with spirituality and nobility, the colour connected with magic, wizardry and the mystical world. Purple is precious and rare – it's a colour that seldom appears in nature and so, when it does, it's viewed with respect and admiration. It's not often that you see purple in interiors, but a dollop of purple in a space can beautifully connect us with our own spirituality, inspiring reflection, contemplation and vision.

PANTONE®
2593 U

Brown is a grounding colour, providing the support system in a home. It's solid, immovable and reliable, but can also be stubborn and a little stuck in its ways. An accent of frivolous pink adds a dollop of much-needed excitement in this space.

An interior overrun with purple, however, can result in a little too much contemplation – and so it's best used as an accent, in soft furnishings and accessories (such as glassware and ceramics). The more modern aubergine is sublime when paired with green.

Black

The confrontational character of black is sure to keep you on your decorative toes. A contemporary approach is to temper its dark and at times depressive nature by using matt finishes and rough textures. Treating black in this raw and natural way takes away its dominating edge, softening its intensity in the process.

PANTONE®
PROCESS BLACK

Even so, living with black requires a certain degree of bravery. Black absorbs the energy in a space and can take over from other elements in the room. If you're intending to live with black, it will well and truly become the focus in a room. Its moody nature could also leave you feeling a little low, emotionally drained or downright exhausted. A space filled with bright light will offset its broodiness, however, and used in bite-sized pieces it will set a dramatic tone, making a big statement without the histrionics.

Grey

Synonymous with chilly days and icy terrain, grey doesn't always get a great rap. It's drab, dull and bland, offering nothing much in the way of energy and excitement. Or is it? There are many subtleties to grey and it can take on the attributes of the colour that makes up its tone. A pale blue–grey, for example, adopts the loveliest characteristics of blue – it's relaxing, ethereal and dreamy. Yellow–grey is chirpy, upbeat and full of beans. Black–grey is moody and broody, strong and sophisticated.

PANTONE®
7543 U

And that's the beauty of grey. It's a neutral third party, offering presence without taking any of the attention. In this way, grey is completely without ego. It can be there, working away, without pretence or affectation. Who could ignore its lovely laid-back nature? It's such a fresh alternative to brown (which can be stodgy) or white (which can be barely there).

White

White is uplifting; its pure and buoyant nature makes you feel as though you're floating, suspended above the earth and weighed down by nothing. A non-competitive colour, white provides an unparalleled backdrop over which to layer a palette that includes any other tone. It's a very accommodating colour to live and work with, allowing the colours around it to shine and prosper.

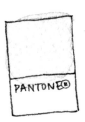

PANTONE®

As a well-considered choice in a palette, white can add an energy and oomph to a scheme, bringing a space to life. If yours is a chilly space graced with little light, stick with warmer whites (those imbued with yellow or brown). A cool grey–white, on the other hand, will chill an overheated room.

Every colour – and even black, grey and white – needs to be respected for its unique attributes and personality traits. Know them well before you employ that colour in your home, to ensure it meets your needs.

LAYER SIX

Bringing in the furniture

Cull before you begin

Edit, edit, edit! Editing is the key to a happy, uncluttered living environment. Go through your possessions at least once a year and cull anything you no longer use by sending it to a grateful home. This will drastically reduce the amount of storage you need in your house and make for easier living in your space.

Storage, storage, storage

Although storage (particularly built-ins) officially falls into the interior design sphere, it's important to cover it here, too. I learnt the hard way the effects of not planning for storage in my home. It was early on, when hubby and I bought our first house (a quaint little fisherman's cottage on the harbour) and we were *sans enfants*, which meant that a little clutter didn't impact too heavily on our day-to-day living. After two children and a few years of collecting stuff, however, things really began to pile up. No built-in storage meant that there was nowhere to put things – and buying storage that's not specifically designed to fit your needs can add just another piece to the pile.

When designing an interior, always include storage, particularly storage that's cleverly divided into drawers, filing cabinets, hanging racks, open shelves and nooks and crannies to fit your way of living and working in your home. If building in your storage, the key is to plan carefully. Begin by searching for storage ideas in magazines and books. Then, with your grid paper and pencils, design a piece that will suit your needs. Design freely to begin with, then once you're happy with the direction, design to scale.

TIP: STORAGE ESSENTIALS

PRACTICAL Go with affordable, easy-to-clean materials such as laminate or a 2pac finish, particularly if you're after a modern and streamlined look.

EASY Choose 'soft-closing' drawers.

NEAT Line your drawers with rubber drawer mats to keep everything in place.

ORGANISED Use labelled storage dividers, such as baskets, crates, boxes, files and so on, to organise the storage compartments. Arrange books on shelves in alphabetical or colour order to make things easier to find.

FUNCTIONAL If you're buying storage that isn't built to fit, then balance and function are the key to choosing a successful piece. Designate a function to your intended piece before you buy and approach it in exactly the same way as you would your built-ins — measuring the cubbyholes and shelving for height, width and depth, and ensuring that your plates, glassware or linen will all fit neatly.

Choosing furniture

Think about shape, comfort and durability. I look to the architecture of a home as my guide when choosing large items such as sofas. Is your house modern and clean-lined? Then go for modern shapes, with streamlined armrests and sturdy cushion backing. If, however, yours is an ornate terrace house with decorative mouldings and pressed metal, then your sofa or armchair, even the legs on your coffee table, can reflect this voluptuousness.

The architecture-to-furniture rule is a great guide for you to start with, but you can, of course, push the envelope here. A mid-century modern home can be filled with mostly clean-lined furniture but with a decorative element or two. This is, after all, what makes a home interesting.

Think about how you plan to live with or on the piece of furniture. What attributes must it embody? How will you interact with it? What kind of personality do you want to create in your space and how will the shape and size of your furniture help create this feeling?

Making your furniture fit

Bring in the furniture in stages — starting with the larger items and working through to the smaller. This ensures that your big furniture items fit snugly into your space, and then you can fill the gaps around them as necessary.

Living room

Is your living room for sitting or lying in? Is it the entertainment hub in your home or is it more of a library? Or is it both? A living room designed for comfort needs wide, comfy sofas and day beds. L-shaped sofas mean there's room enough for everyone to lounge around, but if your space isn't big enough, invest in the widest and deepest sofa your space will allow and, if you can, pair it with two upholstered armchairs. For the ultimate in comfort, keep the fabrics laid-back (linen is perfect).

If a room to sit and converse in is more your speed, consider upright sofas with tufted details and a sculptural chaise longue. Go for luscious fabrics, such as velvet and silk, that evoke a sense of formality and poise. Place the furniture so it's all facing inwards, divided only by a neat coffee table.

Each piece of furniture must have a relationship to the others – meaning they're not too widely spaced. At the other end of the scale, a cramped lounge room with no free-flowing passageways creates a clogged space with little air or energy flow. If yours is a small space, then furniture to scale will ensure you retain all-important balance in the room.

Sofa

There are just two furniture elements that it's crucial to get right – the first is your bed but a very close second comes the sofa. We use sofas to relax, entertain, eat and contemplate our lives. They're the cornerstone of any lounge room, so choosing your sofa should be taken very seriously. The main focus should be comfort. The shape, depth and make-up of your sofa should inspire a lounging feeling. Could there be anything more stressful than a mean sofa that forces you to sit upright rather than relax?

The filling you choose for your cushions will play an integral part in how your sofa feels. Cushions filled only with foam are clean-lined, sturdy and slightly unforgiving, but work well on a modern sofa that needs to keep its shape. Feather and down or feather and down mixed with fibre is more comfortable, but requires regular 'fluffing'.

Measure the piece before you buy and ensure it will fit the intended space. Choose the best quality item your budget will allow; a quality sofa with a sturdy frame and well-made cushions can and will last a lifetime. If you choose wisely, it can be a one-off investment that may only need a re-covering or two in the future.

Your sofa becomes the focus in a living room, so why not go for one that's worthy of all the attention. Remember, though, that even the most glamorous sofa must inspire lounging – and so consider comfort as well as aesthetics when making your choices.

Modular sofas

Life changes and over time so do your furniture needs. I'm all for buying furniture that functions in more than one way — and this idea is particularly pertinent to the sofa. It's always worth considering furniture that gives you future options. A modular sofa makes sense if you see your life changing over time — you're thinking about children, or about moving into a larger house. Modular sofas tend to come streamlined — and so are ideal for a home with a modern aesthetic. They also allow you to change the arrangement of your lounge room — an L-shaped sofa can become two single sofas or a modular sofa can be dissected into one large sofa, one small sofa and an armchair, or possibly two armchairs and a day bed.

Sofas and storage

Any piece of furniture that comes with an added storage option is a winner in my book. A sofa or ottoman that offers storage under the cushion is a worthy choice, particularly if yours is a house filled with toys and magazines. If you're building in indoor or outdoor bench seats, always factor in extra storage — you'll be grateful you did.

TIP: CHOOSING A SOFA WISELY

You can't order in a sample of a sofa, but you can try this. Measure out the dimensions of your sofa of choice — length, width, depth and height — then lay out pieces of newspaper to size, or use milk crates, floor cushions and so on to get to the right height. This will help ensure that the scale of the sofa fits the room comfortably.

The longevity of your sofa (and armchairs) hinges on the quality of the framework housed beneath the cushions and fabric. Ask for an inside view of your sofa before you buy (particularly if you're spending up big). Many sofa makers will have an example of their framework system on view — and it's worth heading to their showroom to check it out. Have them walk you through their manufacturing process. What do they use to construct the framework? Are the pieces glued, stapled (not so sturdy) or screwed together? Are they using a good-quality hardwood to make the base? Try to lift the sofa — the weightier it is, the better made it is.

'Try before you buy' is the motto to bear in mind when searching for sofas. Lying, lounging, sitting and squatting are to be encouraged when you're in store, to ensure you purchase the sofa that fits your needs perfectly.

Armchairs

Every home deserves at least one armchair. A comfortable armchair is the ideal piece upon which to relax, particularly if your armchair comes with an oversized ottoman. You can afford to 'cut loose' with an armchair, going against the grain of your general room scheme with a piece that's quirky and a little offbeat — its scale will never overwhelm a space as a quirky sofa would. This maintains the balance of a space while ensuring it isn't dull. An ornate Louis-type armchair (covered in a bright or highly patterned fabric), for example, will spice up a modernist space, while a textured armchair — such as one in rattan or a Lloyd Loom complete with comfortable cushions — adds a textural element to the room. The key with armchairs is that you're free to experiment.

Coffee table

With a coffee table you can afford to play around with design, shape and material. A hard-edged, rectangular sofa, for example, can be softened by a circular coffee table, while a sofa covered in soft and flowing linen might pair well with an industrial-style coffee table. A nest of coffee tables — two or three tables stacked one on top of the other — adds a quirky element but is also multifunctional. Bear in mind that your coffee table can also function as a storage piece, with hidden shelves and drawers for magazines, newspapers and cushions.

Side tables

These act as end pieces and a kind of framework in a space. Placed at either side of a sofa or bed, they bring the larger item into focus. Determine whether or not your side tables need to be functional or purely decorative. If functional, you'll need to consider what you want to store in them. Will they also be magazine racks or bookshelves? Will they house photo albums or DVDs and CDs? The design of your side tables should reflect these needs with drawers, cubicles and open racks. Also consider whether your table needs a lamp — if so, its top needs to be large enough to support a lamp neatly. If storage isn't an issue, you can afford to choose creatively — one-of-a-kind stools, decorative drums and pedestal tables are all interesting alternatives.

Mix furniture shapes to keep the floor plan interesting. Here, the rectangular sofas, coffee and dining table mix perfectly with curvy armchairs and dining chairs, and circular lighting and accessory options.

Dining room

Are you big on entertaining at home? Do you imagine hours around the dining table celebrating with friends? Are yours large or more intimate gatherings? Will you need to squeeze as many chairs around a dining table as possible or is less more for you? If you're big on celebrating, then comfortable dining chairs are the key to ensuring your gatherings last the distance. Wide upholstered chairs (ideally with arms) will make for a relaxed environment and inspire long lunches and extended dinners. If yours is a small-scale space, however, you need to stick to a petite table and fewer chairs so that you don't spoil the ambience. Ensuring easy movement around the table is the key to comfort. Benches are ideal in this instance, as they can be pushed under the table when the night is done. Stackable chairs that you can leave in the corner are another great space-saver.

Dining table

A dining table serves both a functional and an aesthetic role in a room. Functionally, you need a table that's easy to fit a chair under, that can seat family and friends comfortably, and that fits neatly into the space for which it's intended. Aesthetically, it can add some textural and sculptural interest to the room through its materials and design. A large oak dining table lends warmth to an oversized space, adding a rustic, farmhouse flavour. A circular or oval table, complete with pedestal leg and marble (or laminate) top, creates a sleek, modernist aesthetic and is ideal for cosy nooks and city pads. A circular design can be an architectural reprieve in a square, boxy, well-lit space that suffers from too many right angles. A light, blond-wood table with polite, clean-lined legs gives a home a light, Nordic flavour.

A dining table with options to expand is sensible if yours is a small space and your table only occasionally needs to grow in order to entertain guests. There are a number of ways to change the configuration of your table. You can buy one with fold-down sides, but the downside is that your table will usually have its sides folded down and this can create messy lines. Some tables pull apart at the middle, with a spare piece of table brought out of hiding from underneath when required. But the most basic option is to have a spare top (made from laminate, timber or even an old door) on hand that you can place on top of your existing table and then whisk back into storage afterwards.

Mix and match furniture styles — modern, vintage, classics — to create a space with a personality all its own. This array of dining chairs, for example, adds an eclectic eccentricity to the space.

Dining chairs

Follow the style, scale and form of your dining table in your chairs, to ensure their scale is balanced. The chairs should reflect the design qualities of the table – so a fine, streamlined chair, for example, should accompany a table with fine legs and a streamlined top, while solid, chunky chairs need a solid, chunky table otherwise they're overwhelming. A circular or oval table pairs perfectly with curvy-backed chairs (such as the classic Thonet Café Daum chairs). Industrial metal-legged chairs are ideal for a recycled table. A country-style timber table works well with wicker or Lloyd Loom chairs. Grand armchairs at either end of the table – with matching armless chairs running down each side – make an imposing statement. Mixing and matching dining chairs around the same table adds a quirky interest and gives purpose to what might otherwise be a disparate collection.

TIP: DINING CHAIR ESSENTIALS

Ensure your dining chairs are not too upright – and that the back is not too high – otherwise yours won't be a relaxing dinner. Ideally, the back of a chair should sit somewhere around the middle of your back to ensure adequate support but still allow for movement. Never skimp on the seat – it needs to be wide or round enough to sit on comfortably for an extended period.

Stools

If you're after a uniform feel, your stools can be from the same collection as your dining chairs, or you can mix things up by going for an eclectic stool style and profile. Streamlined plywood stools add texture to a modern interior. Metal stools are sturdy and blend well in an industrial environment. Stools with padded and upholstered seats provide comfort all the way. The key when purchasing a stool is to ensure the seat is large enough to sit on comfortably for extended periods, and that there's a bar between the legs to rest your feet on.

Stools around a kitchen bench are a great way to inspire connection between family and friends. Ensure your stools are sturdy and comfy enough to support all shapes and sizes.

Office station

Now, I do know that these days many of us need to work from home and space can be an issue – but, please, please, please avoid computer stations in bedrooms. Nothing is better at destroying good energy, yours or the bedroom's. Such things are best kept for living spaces or, better still, a dedicated working nook.

When choosing a workstation, go for one that's multifunctional and has some storage. After all, there's nothing more overwhelming than a workstation that can't be seen due to a thick coating of paperwork! An under-bench filing cabinet or sturdy shelves for a line of folders is a key component.

Think about the ergonomics your workstation offers before you invest – what will you be doing at your desk and how do you need to sit there? Will you use it all day or only now and then? If there are two of you at the desk, consider the distance between you – a table too wide will disconnect you from your partner, whereas a table not wide enough will be cramped. Ideally, a computer placed at your natural eye level will prevent you from straining your neck. And importantly, your chair should properly support the weight of your body – with a high enough back.

Bedroom

We spend a lot of our life in bed, so it makes sense to infuse as much comfort and interest into our bedroom space as possible. A large four-poster bed replete with timber frame and bedhead makes an imposing statement, implying that the bedroom is as much a castle as a place of rest. A bed of this scale takes up much of the space in a room and becomes the single focus. A simple upholstered bedhead, on the other hand, can either invoke fun and frivolity (if you choose a bright, patterned fabric) or a laid-back groove (with a loose linen covering, for example). An ornate, tufted bedhead is both grand and feminine, particularly if covered in a luscious velvet or delicate silk.

A bedhead upholstered in simple, natural linen creates a neutral backdrop upon which to layer bed linen of all colours and styles, and allows you to mix and match on a whim and to suit the changing seasons.

In the bedroom, the placement of the furniture is just as important as the furniture itself. You want to create good energy, so place the bed to give you a view out a window and onto the landscape beyond, if possible. A complete wall, rather than one dissected by doors, is important in creating balance and grace. Oversized rooms benefit from a reading nook, styled with a single armchair, side table and reading lamp to fill the space.

LAYER SEVEN

Choosing
fabrics

Upholstery fabrics

The fabrics you choose for your upholstery (for your sofa, chairs, cushions and curtains) are what really make a space sing. Fabric is the life of the decorating party, adding energy and interest, and stamping your home with flavour and personality. It's through fabric that you can add a personal touch to your space, so it's important to get your choices and combinations right. Often, the difficulty is that there's so much to choose from, but understanding the feeling you're trying to create will narrow the options considerably. Every fabric evokes a particular emotion, so the first step is choosing a fabric that reflects how you want to feel in your space.

If you're after a high-end, dramatic interior with a sense of glamour and bling, then you should avoid linens, which are relaxed and laid-back. Instead, you should head straight for the brocades, velvets and silks. If retro-modern is the look you want, then strong, graphic geometrics in bold colours and shapes are the direction for you.

TIP: UPHOLSTERY THAT LASTS

For an indication of how sturdy and long-lasting your fabric will be, check the fabric classification called 'rubs'. The rub number literally indicates how many times you can 'rub' a fabric before it gives way, so the higher the rub number, the more robust the fabric. Commercial-grade fabrics with a rub number between 30 000 and 100 000 are ideal for sofas, armchairs and day bed cushions — the kind of furniture you lie around on. The rub count need not be so high for window treatments or cushions, as you'll rarely come into contact with these items in the same way you would a sofa or chair.

Upholstery styles

When researching, deciding what you want and talking to your upholsterer, it will be useful to know the options available. They include:

TUFTED SOFAS AND ARMCHAIRS   The classic tufted sofa or armchair comes with rolled arms and studded trim – think brown leather Chesterfields. These are heavy, masculine pieces that work well in both a cosy library-style space and an open industrial-style loft. Upholstery in a soft velvet or tight-weave linen adds a feminine feel, while simple tufting on a streamlined, modern piece creates a bridge from the old world to the new.

LOOSE COVERING   Loose-covered sofas lend a space a relaxed, carefree feel. Available in a snug or flowing fit, loose covers not only look contemporary but are just so easy to whip off and clean. This makes them the ideal choice if yours is a many-person household, particularly if there are littlies around. Aesthetically, loose covers work in a holiday-style environment, such as a beach or country house, and are ideal in linens and cotton fabrics. Loose covers are the perfect option if you prefer a light-coloured fabric that's prone to marking and thus requires regular washing.

PLEATED AND GATHERED SKIRTS   If you go for sofa skirting, the style you choose is as important as the fabric and furniture shape. The skirt adds to the overall effect, giving the piece style and personality. A ruffled or gathered skirt has a fuller and fussier profile, making it a more decorative and feminine option. A pleated skirt is a more formal look; structured and precise, it's ideal paired with rolled arms and wingbacks. A straight skirt is a more modern, streamlined option; it has no pleating but is generally separated from the sofa by a row of piping. Straight skirts look great on sofas with little in the way of detail – those with upright, straight-edged backs and sharp arms.

PIPED ARMS AND CUSHIONS   These add an extra aesthetic dimension to your sofa and pair beautifully with tufting. Piping is particularly effective when you go for a different colour from the rest of the sofa – cream, green or pink piping on a chocolate-coloured linen sofa, for example, adds flavour and interest. Self-piping – that is, with piping in the same fabric as the main upholstery – creates definition and an air of formality. For more on cushion piping and trims, see 'Cushions' on page 171.

French-style sofas such as this, with timber detail and precious silk upholstery, are ideal for sitting rather than lying. Adorned with embroidered, elaborately tasselled cushions, this makes a beautiful feature piece.

Fabric types

Use the internet to investigate what the different fabric companies have on offer (for more, see 'Navigating Fabric Showrooms' on page 141). You may also find this guide to styles and weaves useful:

LINEN   Strong and durable but with a soft and fluid finish, linen is ideal for chair and sofa upholstery, particularly as loose covers. It's also great for curtains, cushions, throws and bedspreads. Linen comes in various grades and weaves – loose weaves are best for curtaining and soft furnishings; heavier weaves are ideal for upholstery.

SILK   A delicate fabric with a grand and luscious effect, silk adds depth and glamour to all rooms, particularly when used for curtains and offset with matching scatter cushions. It's an ideal fabric for less frequented areas such as bedrooms. Silk is prone to fading, so always back your silk curtains – or restrict them to windows that see little in the way of direct sunlight.

COTTON   A knockabout fabric, ideal for living areas and children's playrooms, cotton is versatile, durable and breathable (due to its unique fibre structure). It's ideal for everything from bedding to curtains and soft furnishings. Cottons (particularly the thicker ones) evoke a laid-back, unpretentious feel and work beautifully in family homes, as they're so rough and tumble and easily washable. Sturdy cotton drills are ideal for outdoor use (but shouldn't be left out in the weather).

BROCADE   This highly decorated fabric, woven to give an embossed, self-patterned effect, is often made using silk. Rich and luscious (and expensive), brocades add a layer of depth and artistry when applied to a single item such as a cushion or ornamental throw. You'll find brocades in old-world interiors, but with the right patterning and colour way they work just as well in a modern environment.

VELVET   The smooth, shiny and luscious texture of velvet makes a dramatic statement in the home. The most beautiful of all seem to be liquid, with a finish that moves as you do, appearing light and reflective one minute and then deep and dark the next. Velvet is lovely when used to upholster a sofa (as for my beautiful peacock blue–green sofa on page 186), or for drapery or a cushion or two or three. Velvet in jewel colours is a deep and dramatic pairing of colour and texture, whereas hot pink or bright yellow velvets add fun to an otherwise sophisticated fabric.

WOOL Roughly textured and very warm, wool in throw rugs and cushions makes a lovely accompaniment to both cotton and linen upholstery. Unless you don't mind a little itching and scratching, avoid woolly furniture upholstery! Knitted woolly furnishings, however, particularly in a natural colour palette, help create an interesting and textural interior.

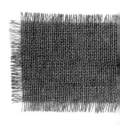

HEMP A more popular choice in recent years with the rise of the eco movement, hemp is an interesting textured fabric that's beautiful in hand-dyed natural colour ways and organic block prints. Choose hemp for accessory pieces – such as sofa and floor cushions or ottomans – rather than upholstery, as it frays easily and is highly textured. Hemp is perfect paired with linen and cotton, adding a whole layer of texture and pattern.

JUTE Also called hessian, jute is similar to hemp in that it's roughly textured and organic in nature and plays beautifully in the eco aesthetic. Often used to make sacks, these days jute has been cannily repurposed for funky home furnishings.

LEATHER Think Chesterfield leather chairs – those brown, worn-in leather armchairs often found in men's clubs and libraries – and you have leather at its finest and most traditional. These days, however, you can find leather dyed in any colour and used on ottomans, cushions, sofas and armchairs. Leather is a durable, easy-care fabric, ideal for high-traffic areas, but still soft, natural and comfortable. Whether a piece upholstered in leather is contemporary or traditional depends more on its shape and style than the leather itself – rolled arms and wingbacks fall into the traditional category, while streamlined shapes and sharp edges make for a modern leather piece.

SUEDE This is leather with a brushed rather than smooth finish, giving it a slightly textured, more dappled effect. A popular choice for sofas, armchairs, ottomans and the occasional throw cushion, suede is soft, comfortable and durable, although prone to losing its brushed finish in places.

Fabric texture

We interact with our fabrics on many levels. Initially we react to them on an aesthetic level, as we're drawn to their colour, pattern and style. But possibly more important is how a fabric feels to the skin. We sit, sleep and lounge on every fibre of fabric, so if we're to be truly comfortable on an item of furniture, the fabric has to be just right.

You must feel at one with your decorating fabrics, and this means you need to put as much effort into choosing texture as you do colour and pattern. The texture you choose will play a large part in how you feel in your home, but a texture that works for one person will be completely wrong for another. My gorgeously sublime peacock-green velvet sofas, for example, make me feel as though I'm lounging upon liquid gold. For me, they're luscious, matriarchal and self-confident – in the lap of velvet I feel sublimely feminine. Hubby, on the other hand, views sitting on velvet as akin to hanging out at his granny's house, which for him means feeling old-fashioned, a little musty, and as though ants are crawling all over his skin!

How could the same fabric evoke such deeply differing reactions? Therein lies the power of texture, and so it's important to choose wisely. Texture can make or break whether an interior is liveable. It could be beautiful, yes, but liveable?

Here are a few guidelines for thinking about texture. They're by no means hard and fast, but they're a good starting point:

RELAXED   You can't beat linen if you want a fabric that evokes a relaxing feeling. It's the epitome of sophisticated relaxation but also the ultimate in loose and laid-back, and the finer the linen, the looser and more flowing it will be. Linen is divine to sit, read, eat and sleep on – and works as everything from a loose cover on a sofa to bedclothes. Soft, smooth and tactile, linen is an easy fabric to live with, and doesn't irritate the skin. This is no cheap and cheerful fabric, however, so to ensure you don't break the bank, be absolutely certain about how and where you want to use it.

GLAMOROUS   What could be more glamorous than deep, rich, layered, smooth and sensuous velvet? Velvet is a feminine fabric, but it's no girl – it's woman all the way. It should be reserved for special items in a room that deserves glamour – a favourite chair, bedroom drapes or a feature cushion on your treasured sofa. The colour of velvet changes as you move on it, and the depth and intensity of the plush pile alters as you lounge.

The texture of a fabric plays as important a role as its colour and pattern – it defines how you feel living in a space. To ensure you'll be comfortable living together, interact with your fabrics before you make your final choices – this means sitting, lying and rolling on them, if need be!

ROUGH AND READY   Jute, hessian and rustic and rough cottons –
these fabrics mean business and are ideal for cushions, ottomans,
throws and floor rugs. Adding a natural, textural dimension to a space,
they're like living with the outdoors inside, and you can rough and
tumble them with no adverse effect. Textured in the real sense of the
word, at their extreme they're itchy, scratchy and not for the faint
of heart.

COUNTRY RUSTIC   Chenille, corduroy and heavy cotton are
hardwearing, rustic fabrics that offer grunt in the way of texture and
interest but are still soft and welcoming to the skin. For me, they're
masculine in nature; heavy-set and all-embracing, they envelop you,
comfort you, lull you to sleep. They're soft to the skin but not in the
same relaxed, carefree way as, say, linen. They're more 'definite' in that
they're not flimsy and flowing but are weighty, meaty fabrics – salt of
the earth, if you like. Often, you'll find fabrics of this kind in a warm
and inviting ski lodge or a library or men's club, perhaps. In deep
colours, such as chocolate brown and dark purples, they're fabrics
not to be messed with.

FORMAL   Patterned jacquards, brocades, velvets and silks all offer
subtle shine and softness with a touch of sophisticated sparkle. They're
special, not-to-be-used-daily fabrics, the ones you'll find in the formal
dining and sitting rooms of classical houses. Swathe your interior in
these upper-class fabrics and you'll feel a little upper-class yourself,
but they're best avoided if you're the lounging type or you have
littlies around.

FEMININE   Soft silk mixed with loose linen is a gentle mix of
a natural, slightly more rustic texture and a smooth, shimmery texture.
It makes for feminine fabrics, especially when paired with a palette of
barely-there neutrals and muted pink, salmon or icy-blue tones.

TIP: CAN YOU LIVE WITH THAT FABRIC?

Always put your fabric through the feel test by investing in a metre or two and living
with it for a few weeks or so. Lie on it, roll on it, sleep on it. Ask yourself how you
feel around it. Could you live with it for an extended period of time? Successful
design hinges not only on how a piece looks to the eye but also how that piece feels
to the skin, so make sure you really can live with it.

This curtain fabric lends
a sense of flow and movement
to the space, through its use of
pattern, style and weight. It also
provides sufficient privacy without
blocking the view beyond.

Fabric pattern

The 'wow' in your interior comes courtesy of pattern. Pattern really gets a space jumping, bringing it to life and injecting style, flavour and character in a way no other element can. Viewing pattern as a kind of artwork in your interior will make it easier to come to terms with the numerous options. What kind of artwork are you most attracted to? What colours and forms do you feel most excited by?

Perhaps your heart skips a beat at the sight of a Matisse? If so, a cacophony of colour brought together in broad brushstrokes and loose, organic detail could be the direction for you. If you're into Miró, geometric shapes and sharp lines in bright primary colours could be the right direction. A love of Paul Gauguin suggests deep, muted colour in rich organic shapes. Or perhaps you're more attracted to black-and-white photography, in which case solid blocks of tone on tone could be your starting point.

As with all elements of design, the key is to find a direction and move towards it. Once you have a broad idea of what kind of pattern works for you, you can begin the process of editing the options. This will help you avoid the trap of turning up to a fabric showroom without a purpose or a plan. Instead, take your edited ideas with you and use them as a starting point. If, during the process, you find yourself organically moving in the opposite direction, then go with the flow – you never know where you might end up!

Pattern types

FREE-FORM AND ORGANIC Free-form pattern is soft-edged, loose and carefree, with a random, organic feel. Often with a screen-printed or hand-sketched design, these patterns are ideal for laid-back, relaxed interiors with an eco or natural flavour. They work well when paired with warm timber tones to evoke the feeling of living amongst nature.

MODERN GEOMETRIC Clean, sharp lines with solid blocks of colour create bold styles that work perfectly in a Danish or Modern environment. Think the 1960s and 1970s: hot pink, notice-me yellow and punchy green with blocks of black are the 'don't be afraid' colours you'll find in the geometric realm. Pare back the clean lines with softer, more muted colour and you have a modern take on an older style – as embodied by the enduringly popular Marimekko fabrics (see 'Suppliers' on page 200).

STRIPES   Although geometric, stripes deserve a class of their own as the options are so numerous and broad. Stripes range from bold varieties – wide, awning-style stripes in strong, extrovert colour – to softer, more organic treatments – such as ticking – and a mixture of the two, which is relaxed but still makes a statement. Stripes offer an easy way to introduce patterning and pair beautifully with both a simple solid and a more complex floral or paisley.

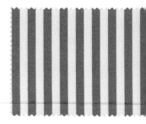

CHECKS   Strong geometric undertones are coupled with interest and detail in checked fabrics, which range from simple two-coloured cottons and linens to the more complex colour combinations you'll find in textured wool or silk tartans and plaids. The simpler the colour way, the more relaxed the pattern, while deep shades and multi-colouring create a complex pattern that adds strength and focus to a room.

REPETITIVE   Repetitive patterning provides a kind of structure to your space – there's nothing random about a drawing or icon that's deliberately positioned to provide a kind of order. Repetitive patterning is definitive, neat, tidy and in its place, but you can loosen up the idea by going for a repeated free-form drawing rather than a clean and sharp option. It works particularly well in children's rooms, where it's just as important to provide some sense of order as aesthetic interest.

FLORAL   Floral patterning comes in such a broad range of approaches that there's surely a style to suit any overall scheme, whether the fabric is sharp-lined and modern or older-style chintz. Floral fabrics run the gamut from block-printed native wattle to a pretty rose design in broad, loose brushstrokes and formal botanicals that are drawn 'just so'. They add a kind of English majesty to a room, even if you go for more relaxed hand-painted florals in brighter, more modern tones. Every room can cope with a floral touch, even if it's just one cushion.

TOILE   Depicting pastoral scenes – a picnic in the park, a promenade through the garden, a peasant at work – toile fabrics are from a bygone era and pair perfectly with French-inspired interiors. Toiles come in one colour (often a rich deep red or blue) drawn on a natural linen-coloured backdrop. To enjoy the full effect of toile, the key is to show as much of the scene as possible.

TRIBAL   A mix of geometric patterning and organic, hand-drawn, hand-woven and hand-dyed designs, tribal patterns are based on traditional stories and design fundamentals, and so are a decorative chronicle of the life and times of the people who created them. Tribal patterning is deep, earthy and earnest, as much about history as decoration – think ikat, suzani and kilim floor rugs (see pages 182–84).

Applying pattern

As a general rule, we tend to upholster the larger items of furniture in plain, solid colours – unless you're a very confident decorator who's prepared to take the creative leap. Solid base colours protect us from investing in an expensive pattern that we may quickly tire of. And keeping it solid on the big-ticket items opens up the opportunity to play around with the detail without the stress.

Here are a few other ideas for introducing pattern. Playing around with the options and adding an element of surprise will keep the space fresh.

CUSHIONS   To create a layered interior with interest and excitement, choose cushions (including floor cushions, day bed cushions and bolsters) in a variety of patterns that all work in the same colour scheme. Go for a boxed cushion for the floor and day bed and employ two patterned fabrics, one for the top and bottom of the cushion and another for the sides. Ditto with the bolsters. Or think patchwork for a crazy, one-of-a-kind pattern. As cushions are relatively inexpensive, you can afford to experiment a little, so if you see a bold fabric you love, take the leap. (For more on cushions, see page 171.)

OTTOMANS   Smaller than an armchair but larger than a cushion, an ottoman provides the ideal opportunity to introduce an interesting pattern to an otherwise simple, understated room. If you're going for a relaxed ottoman style, say with a loose cover, seek relaxed patterns that complement this look – such as hand-drawn or hand-painted striped, checked or organic patterns. A fully upholstered ottoman, on the other hand, requires a more structured print, in a sharp geometric or repetitive tribal pattern. Think outside the square a little – why not upholster your ottoman in a patterned kilim rug or an antique suzani fabric, or in a mix-and-match of vintage tea towels or jute coffee sacks.

BEDSPREADS AND THROWS   A patterned bedspread or throw is a major piece of patterning in a room – the scale of the fabric on even a single bed will naturally draw the focus away from most other pieces. If you're going for a strong pattern on the bed, keep the patterning to a minimum on your other pieces. If you do want to infuse more patterning, choose a plainer geometric with simple shape and colour to reinforce the pattern on the bed rather than detract from it. A bedspread in a less intrusive fabric – a simple French-inspired striped linen, say – can cope with more pattern, on the curtains, armchair and cushions. A natural choice is an unobtrusive floral in muted tones that blend harmoniously with the simplicity of the fabric on the bed.

CURTAINS AND BLINDS Patterned curtains and blinds will become the focus in the room, so keep the patterning in the rest of the room to a minimum. A cushion here or there, or a small ottoman, will be an ideal accompaniment. If, however, the pattern is a simple one, add another complementary pattern to spice things up. Check that the pattern runs down the fabric roll to give a nice long drop that doesn't require any joins, and make a note of the fabric width before you buy, to ensure it's appropriate for the width of your window. (For more on curtains and blinds, see 'Natural Light' on pages 148–50.)

Clashing pattern and colour can be the very elements that underpin an eclectic interior. Here, the muted colour tones provide a common thread between the soft furnishings. Add to this a harmonious blend of large-scale and small-scale block and detailed pattern, and you have busy patterning that retains a sense of balance.

Patterning a room

First decide just how much pattern you want in your space. Do you intend to pattern sparsely — perhaps a cushion or two to combine with otherwise block colour? Or is a scattering of pattern more your style — patterned curtains, cushions and rug, for example? Or are you the all-out-pattern kind of decorator, throwing together different patterns in the curtains, sofas, rug and cushions in a crazy mishmash of colour and design?

I like pattern in its place, as a definite feature in the room but with a fairly clear position — in a floor rug, say, and a cushion or two. Too much pattern sends me into a cleaning and organising spin, as I try to create some order among the conflicting colours and shapes. Not enough pattern and I feel a little bored, lacking life and energy.

The key is to work it to your taste and, as with each element of design, to consider its balance in the room. Any pattern or patterns you use should appear at either end of the space — adding their personality to all areas of the room rather than all on their lonesome in only one. The pattern you use for the curtains should appear at least once or twice in the cushions. The pattern on the ottoman should appear in a cushion or throw. However, applying a bold, one-of-a-kind pattern to one armchair only could turn it into statement piece. Analyse your space with a critical eye — are there enough patterns for your taste or too many?

TIP: CHOOSING AND COMBINING PATTERNS

When patterning a room, begin by choosing the pattern for the largest pieces of furniture in the space, such as the sofa, bed or windows. Once you've found these patterns and know their colour and strength, you can choose your patterns for the smaller items so that they work in harmony. Choosing a bolshie fabric for a cushion as your starting point means you're working backwards in the room, trying to match your major pieces to your smallest, which makes the job of patterning a little trickier. As always, however, the rules are made to be broken. If you come across a cushion you love and simply can't live without, you could use its pattern as the springboard to your whole interior scheme. As you become more confident with your decorating skills, you'll feel freer to push the boundaries, which makes for an exciting interior that's always on its toes.

Blend patterns of the same genre for a harmonious space. This room combines geometric, block and repetitive patterning, all with Middle Eastern overtones.

EXERCISE: Pattern 1, 2, 3

Begin the process of patterning with your colour scheme handy. This will generally consist of at least three colours — the base colour/s and one to three highlight colours. Choose one or two of your highlight colours then head directly to this colour section in the fabric showroom (see 'Navigating Fabric Showrooms', opposite). Spend time sifting through and finding patterns that fit in with the overall artistic theme you're trying to create — organic, geometric, and so on. Pick out a couple of different patterns to begin with — say, a floral and a stripe — and play around with them. Do they work together? Is their scale complementary? An overly wide stripe and a tiny floral may not make the best of friends, for example, so pair the boldness of the stripe with a large-brushstroke floral instead. As is always the case with fabric, colour and pattern, ask for a sample, take it home and drape it over your furniture. Look at it, lie on it, live with it. Wait a few days. Are you in love? If so, go for it. Or is something not quite right? In which case, back to the drawing board.

TIP: MAKING PATTERN WORK

Patterning in layers is a good way to begin. Start with the boldest and largest patterns (say, a wide stripe) then choose the more decorative partners. Solid colours or more solid patterns work best as the backdrop, while smaller patterns and stripes (such as ticking) are best at the front. As always, start large at the back and work towards small at the front. As you become more confident, you'll naturally mix it all up for interest's sake, giving your interior an eclectic edge and creating a lived-in, light-hearted atmosphere.

Navigating fabric showrooms

Decorating a home is as much about editing as anything else, and at its core, navigating the fabric showroom is an exercise in sifting through the options (see 'Suppliers' on page 200 for some possible starting points).
The key is to arm yourself with a plan before stepping out the door:

1   **GO GENTLY**   Tackle your showroom visits in stages. The first round of visits should be a research mission only – scan what's available and get a broad sense of your aesthetic direction. It's worth gathering swatches at this stage, but don't worry if you don't yet have creative clarity – use what you're naturally drawn to as a guide.

2   **DO YOUR RESEARCH**   After your first visit, use the internet and blogs to sift through the various collections on offer. Each collection has been designed with a style in mind: some will be glamorous and sophisticated, others relaxed and carefree, still others a combination of the two. With a little research, it will become clear which collections speak to you. Make a note of those you love and print out examples. Combining your finds in a folder is a great way to keep organised.

3   **KNOW YOUR MIND**   Head out again, this time with conviction, armed with your plan or scheme and a list of the collections you like. Fabric showrooms are organised in two ways – by brand and by colour. If you're working to a colour scheme, head straight to that section. Pull the fabrics out. Lay them on the table. Ask for help from the showroom assistant. Once you've narrowed it down to a few colours, begin weeding through the collections you like. This is where it's easy to be swayed, so keep your colour scheme in mind at all times. At the same time, retain an open mind, as the fabric you end up choosing is not always the one you intended.

4   **COLLECT SWATCHES**   Always ask for swatches of the fabrics you like. Sometimes, the showroom will have the swatch you're after on file. Other times, they'll need to order it in. Fabrics from overseas, including swatches, can take up to a month to come in, so bear that in mind in terms of your schedule.

Ordering fabric

The odd fabric and haberdashery showroom will be happy to sell a limited supply direct to the public, but usually only professional decorators and interior designers can order directly from fabric showrooms. With this in mind, you'll need to find yourself a decorator, decorating shop or upholsterer (see below) to order the fabric for you. Many upholsterers and decorators only carry a small number of fabric swatches, waterfalls (fabric drops) and books for you to view, so heading out to the fabric showroom and collecting your swatches before you go to the upholsterer will both give you more options and cut the decision-making time in half.

Fabric prices vary dramatically depending on their weave, colour, pattern and brand, and decorator fabrics are more expensive than off-the-shelf fabrics. What you pay for, however, is not just quality (which tends to be much higher in decorator fabrics) but uniqueness. Depending on the brand, fabrics are generally ordered by the metre or half-metre, but some patterned fabrics designed for curtains and panels will be ordered by the drop.

Finding an upholsterer

Word of mouth is the best way to find a good upholsterer in your area. As soon as you ask around, you'll be amazed by how many recommendations and non-recommendations you get. To be sure you're onto a winner, however, visit your upholsterer's workroom and get a first-hand view of their work. This way you can be as sure as possible that they're the right person for the job. Always get a firm written quote before they begin any work – you'd be surprised how many hidden extras can pop up during the process!

Once your fabric arrives at the workroom and before the upholsterer begins work, always check that the fabric is right and make sure they know which side of it you want facing out. Once upon a time, very early in my career, I learnt this very valuable lesson the hard way! I was having a chair upholstered for a client in a beautifully patterned fabric that I'd ordered and sent directly to the upholsterer without checking first. In my mind, it was obvious which side of the pattern needed to face up (the patterned side!), but the upholsterer had other ideas. The chair came back with the pattern facing inwards, making an unhappy-looking chair and, needless to say, a not-very-happy client.

LAYER EIGHT

Light exactly
where you
need it

Analyse your lighting needs

In reality, you need to assess your lighting throughout the decorating process. At the beginning, as you're creating your concept, you need to analyse how the light works in each room, whether you have enough natural light or too much, whether you need to pump in artificial light and whether or not you can use your furnishings to conceal or highlight the amount of light in a room. Then, as you work through each stage, you need to keep thinking about light, and ask yourself how each decision will affect the light in that room.

If you're renovating a room and starting from scratch with your fixtures, you'll need to think about your architectural lighting – whether you want downlights and from there how many lights the space needs. In the kitchen, for example, you need to ensure there's enough light where you need it, although as downlights in the bathroom can confront rather than conceal, wall lights could be the answer there.

Separate from architectural lighting is decorative lighting – wall lights, pendants, and so on. Use this to manipulate the amount of light in the room, create a warm, cosy corner or illuminate a painting or sculpture.

Spend some time in the space: sit in it, read in it, watch TV in it. How does the light change throughout the day? What do you need the lighting to do for you? Write down your findings. No natural light in your ideal reading nook? Consider a floor lamp with a gooseneck that hangs over your chair, ensuring you have light exactly where you need it. Need general ambience? A series of lamps scattered through the space will create a warm, soft glow in which to relax. Treated with thought, light can add a whole new layer of interest, intrigue and excitement to your interior.

Natural light

The most beautiful, flattering, simultaneously warming and cooling light is natural light. Time spent in a naturally lit environment is the most uplifting of all. We all need some natural light to keep us upbeat and on the pulse. Natural light, particularly the bright, pulsating kind, has a direct effect on how we feel, so you should promote as much natural light in your space as possible.

Monitor your natural light from dawn to dusk, summer to winter, checking how it works during these times – and what kind of light you receive (whether it's warm or cool, with a tinge of orange or of grey–blue). Assess the environment around exterior windows or doors to see what colour of light is being reflected into your space. Do grey-coloured high-rise buildings surround you? Then your light will be affected by this grey cast. Is your environment infused with busy tones of green?

One way to get an insight into what light is doing in a space at any given time of day is to take a snapshot of the room at one- to two-hour intervals. Ensure that your camera is not on flash and that you use the same light settings each time. Download these pictures onto your computer and monitor the changes. Only when you've worked out what the light is doing can you influence the natural light so that it works for you.

While your window treatments are decorative, they're essentially functional, and these two aspects must work in tandem. To brighten up an otherwise dull space, use light-coloured furnishings, ensuring they're in the direct path of the light source, natural or artificial. Using the furnishings as a light reflector like this is a great way to 'bounce' light and warmth into the room. Shiny materials, such as metallics and silks, also work well as light reflectors, so consider these options for details such as cushions. For a low-lit space, always keep your window treatments to transparent fabrics – as the last thing it needs is a heavy curtain or blind blocking out the light source. Sheer curtains in muslin or voile, or a textured alternative such as netting or a loose knit, are great options. A single lace panel also works well, providing privacy without blocking out the light.

If your space has *too much* light, then consider plantation shutters – their louvres give you direct control over how much light enters your space. A sleek, more modern alternative is a Verosol roll-down blind – its UV formulation gently filters the light and offers both shade from the blasting sunshine and protection from its harmful UV rays.

Remember, the light changes depending on your location. Australian light can be bright and sharp, whereas northern European light is softer, with a grey undertone. Always take into account the light in your location when making decorating choices.

CURTAINS   As we've seen, you can diffuse light into a dull room without blocking it out entirely by going for curtains in a transparent fabric such as muslin or voile – or organza if glamour is what you're after. Keep the gathers and folds to a minimum, as the less fabric in the curtain, the more transparent it will be. Alternatively, add more gathers and folds if you want a little less light but don't want to block it out entirely. If you want the best of both worlds, hedge your lighting bets with a double-layered curtain – a transparent voile or muslin underneath, with a heavier opaque fabric layered over the top. If too much sun is the problem, then a heavier fabric (backed with UV protection) will be more suitable for your space.

BLINDS   Using blinds to control the light is an all or nothing kind of affair – they're either up or down, open or closed, so you have less manoeuvrability and thus less subtlety of light. If you want privacy without completely blocking out the view, choose a streamlined metallic blind. If you'd like to add colour and interest as well as block out the light, go for a fabric blind, such as a roman blind. Venetian blinds offer slivers of view with the tilt of a lever while maintaining your privacy.

PLANTATION SHUTTERS   Timber plantation shutters provide a relaxed, laissez-faire look and feel for your windows. They're reminiscent of lazy days by the beach, somewhere beside the aqua-blue waters of the Caribbean. Plantation shutters are a very permanent option for your windows – they're built in to the fabric of the house, which makes them more of an architectural detail than a decorative one. Plantation shutters can come in raw timber or sprayed to a colour, but white is the most popular choice. They look stylish and, apart from being easy to keep clean, they're ideal for controlling light and add a quirky detail to all styles of home.

Artificial Light

Whatever option you choose for your fixed artificial light, have your electrician wire the lights to a dimmer pad, so you have complete control over how much or how little light you allow into your space.

Floor lamps

A floor lamp adds drama to a room — working as both a sculptural feature and a light source. Floor lamps can round out an interior, adding interest and decorative zeal to corners and 'dead' spaces. They're also rather functional, and a delightful light source for reading and intimate endeavours. Think of your floor lamp with this kind of reverence, not just as a superfluous functional item. Choose stands with interesting shapes — a curved gooseneck or tri-leg pedestal, perhaps — in materials such as raw timber, zinc, stainless steel or even ceramic. Then add a shade that complements your overall room scheme and whose shape is in balance with the base. In terms of functionality, the height of your floor lamp is vital, both in terms of being able to sit under it comfortably while reading and its relationship to your other furniture.

Pendant lights

If you're after filtered light from above as an alternative or an addition to downlighting, which can often be harsh and source-specific, think about pendant lighting. When choosing a pendant light (one that hangs from the ceiling on a long cord, adorned by a shade) there are a few things to consider. First, you need to think about placement. Often a pendant will sit above a dining table, or in the centre of the living or dining room as the focus, or in the corner of a room as a sculptural piece.

Wherever a pendant goes, its length, including the shade, is important. In a living room, for example, you could bump your head on a low-hanging pendant every time you're near.

How many pendants you need is another consideration, and this will very much depend on the shade you choose. With a larger, show-stopping shade, you need only one for full impact. A small, organically shaped shade could need some friends — three is generally a good option in this case, but if more are required, an odd number is best for balance.

Floor lamps offer diffused light with a dramatic, often sculptural edge. Choose your lamp based not only on aesthetics but where you like your light to fall. In this photograph, the soft light illuminates this otherwise dark corner to show-stopping effect.

Choose your shade based on the kind of light you'd like in the room. Soft, diffuse light, such as that offered by George Nelson Bubble Lamps, adds a warm glow, while a loosely woven rattan shade will give glow and shadow as the light sneaks out through the cracks in the weave. A chandelier offers dainty light from a number of bulbs — it's pretty, dappled and elegant. A plywood shade with cut-outs and perforation, such as the David Trubridge light series, will provide more definite shadows, casting a kind of moving artwork on the walls. Old-fashioned tin or zinc saucer shades pair a clean-lined shape with a weathered patina, complementing both a French-inspired interior and an otherwise sparse, modern room.

Table lamps

Pair quirky, mismatched lamp bases and shades to create unique lighting features that are not only practical but also decorative.

Ideal perched on bedside tables, sideboards, credenzas and hall or entranceway consoles, table lamps are the ultimate in ambient lighting, as they act less as functional lamps and more to set the mood in a room. With their small scale and soft glow, they create a relaxed kind of atmosphere. And as they're movable items, you can chop and change depending on the mood you're trying to create and where you prefer your ambience.

Be creative with your choice of base and think outside the square to create a unique piece for your interior. Many different vessels can be converted into a lamp base — a retro ceramic vase, a heavy-based glass container or an exotic timber carving — so speak to your electrician about the options for the piece you have in mind. Pair the base with a simple shade and you have a one-of-a-kind creation. If your only option is an off-the-shelf lamp, then be sure to mix and match the style, shape and texture of your base and shade to make your lamp unique.

Lampshades are the icing on the lighting cake — they bring your lamp to life, giving it style and personality. Choose a shade to complement your base, following through with a similar design sensibility from top to bottom. A sleek wooden base pairs perfectly with a clean-lined oval shade covered in a natural, textured material such as bamboo or plywood. An elegant and glamorous art deco chrome base is a natural partner for a symmetrical glass shade. A glass chandelier, whether a small-scale table lamp or a pendant that acts as a focus piece, adds drama, grace and femininity to a room. If laid-back beach style is your preference, go for a shade in textured rattan (or a similar textured fabric).

As always, once you become more confident, turn these design principles on their head. A crazy-patterned lampshade can be paired beautifully with an elegant glass base, while a retro ceramic base works well with a sleek modern circular shade. Playing around with the possibilities is what will add excitement to your space, keep it on its toes and make it sparkle.

Fabric shades, made using one fabric or a mix of fabrics, add colour, texture and pattern in an unusual way. They offer a one-of-a-kind flavour, allowing you to design a piece that works completely with your chosen interior style. Add ribbon or pom-pom detail if you're designing for a child's bed or playroom. Speak to a lampshade supplier and ask for your chosen shade to be supplied 'nude' (without a fabric finish) and have your upholsterer make your shade for you from the fabric you've chosen. Or if you're crafty, you might want to make your own.

Wall lights or sconces

Wall lights are a unique combination of architectural and decorative lighting – while they're part of the fabric of the building, they also serve an ornamental purpose, with their elaborate shapes and shades. I do prefer to integrate lighting into the architecture of a room as much as possible. Although wall lighting is fixed to the wall for good, or at least until you renovate again, it's neat, precise and keeps floors and surfaces free of excess furniture items.

For me, the ultimate in wall lighting is fixed to either side of the bed. This keeps bedside tables free for piles of books and cups of tea, rather than lamp bases and cords. But you can plan wall lighting anywhere, from either side of the front door to a series along the hallway or in the living room or bathroom. Like pendants, wall lights come in many styles, from intricate chandelier drops to those with clean-lined modern arms and shades or pretty floral shades filled with colour and chintz.

You'll need an electrician to wire in your wall lights – and it's best to have them look at your space before you choose your light style, shape and size, to ensure that it's actually possible to install what you have in mind.

Candles

The softest, sweetest and most flattering light of all has to be candlelight. There's nothing I love more than filling a room – bathroom, bedroom, lounge, I'm not fussy – with candles of all sizes, shapes and scents. Soya candles are best as they're non-toxic (with no petroleum additives), have an extended burn time and are less sooty. Choose candles of all shapes and sizes and light them all for full effect – then enjoy as you drift off into candlelight heaven!

Candles become decorative features, particularly when they rest under domes or on elaborate candelabras.

TIP: CHOOSING LIGHT GLOBES

The type of light globe you choose makes a huge difference to the ambience of a space. There are so many light bulbs on the market, sometimes it's difficult to know what should go where. The main decision to make is what you need the space to do for you and how you want the light to make you feel.

Warm light is the loveliest of all, particularly if you want to create a relaxing mood. Bright white light in a lounge or dining space can be too intense, so in these rooms use bulbs with a yellow cast. Employ bright light in the kitchen and bathroom, where you need the cleanest, clearest light to carry out your tasks easily. Downlights or halogens, which offer pure white light, will do the job for you here. Halogens are also a great choice where you don't want the bulb to influence the colour of your furnishings. Fluorescent lights, designed to emulate daylight, are better put-together these days, but their light is still not the most flattering to live with in the home, so they're best kept to laundries, garages and sheds.

Before you buy a light globe, speak with your local lighting shop about the different types they have. They can steer you towards the best bulb for the job and will help you narrow your options. And of course, use energy-efficient bulbs wherever you can.

Choose your light bulbs for their efficiency rating and also for the kind of light they emit – pure, bright white light or a soft yellow light. I always choose yellow light bulbs for mood lighting, such as lamps and pendants in the lounge and bedrooms, and white light for the 'doing' rooms, such as the kitchen and laundry.

LAYER NINE

Accessorising —
the key to
individuality

The finishing touches

How do you feel about your space ? You've certainly done the hard yards – you've planned, devised a concept and measured your space; you've come to terms with colour, paint, furniture, fabric and texture; and you've chosen your lighting. You should be feeling pretty good about your space right now. You've laid the foundations, made some difficult decisions and all in all your space should be looking and feeling exactly as you hoped it would. So what now? Well, now comes the really fun stuff. Yes, if you weren't having fun before, you definitely will be now! Now's the time to accessorise, and with that comes the opportunity to play.

Accessories are the finishing touches in a room – they make a space liveable, cosy, fun and ever so exciting. They turn your very well-decorated house into a very well-decorated home. When designing interiors and styling for interior decorating magazines, I spend a lot of time in other people's houses. And the most extraordinary homes I see are those filled to the brim with accessories of all shapes and sizes – artwork, collections, books and a multitude of beautiful things.

While the furniture and fabrics are the backbone in your interior, giving it a unique stamp and individuality, it's the accessories that make your space a true one of a kind. The artworks you choose for your walls and how you group them in collections, how you fill a vase and the way you put everything together says so much about who you are and your personal journey through life. These are the very things that make a space yours. These are the very things that ensure no two spaces will ever be alike. These are the things that make living in your home a pure joy.

Collecting your accessories

This part of the decorating journey should be a slow and steady process. You should collect the beautiful accessories that adorn your space over time rather than all at once just to fill it up. Pieces bought in bulk to fill up a room will make it seem tokenistic and without depth or body. All good things take time, after all, so don't be in any rush to fill the room. Enjoy the process of collecting your accessories and building your collection piece by piece. Cast a wide net, to ensure your space is varied, eclectic and layered. Draw on your travels and experiences as your style guide — anything you collect while you're travelling will ensure that your home is not only unique but also the storybook of your life and times.

I'm a big one for sourcing local arts and crafts when I travel — I buy ceramics, glassware, wall hangings and artworks wherever I go. These are all easy enough to stuff into your suitcase and bring home into your real life. (If your suitcase gets too full, then there's always the postal service!) This is one sure way of ensuring there'll never be a duplicate of your home anywhere else in the world.

Artwork

At the heart of it, artwork, be it paintings, sculptures, drawings or photographs, adds a sense of creativity and soul to your space. The artwork you're attracted to says a lot about who you are and what you love — it's a wonderful way to add beauty to your walls while also telling the story of your life. Your artwork should be as diverse and layered as you are.

Collecting artwork should really be a lifetime pursuit. As we age and evolve, what we need to surround ourselves with evolves as well. And so an art collection is never truly complete. Collecting art doesn't have to be an expensive, indulgent quest. Beautiful art comes in many shapes and packages. Student artists often create some of the most divine works of all. You can source great student art at end-of-year art college shows for very reasonable prices. If you're lucky, you may just purchase something created by a future artistic great.

Artworks of various sizes, shapes and genres pair well when grouped in a configuration that appears balanced and harmonious. To ensure the best layout, arrange the artworks on the floor first and play around with their positioning.

There are a number of ways to approach the collection of artwork. One is to be guided simply by the work that moves you, regardless of its style, shape or colour palette. This approach works well in an interior where the furnishings are neutral and low-key, allowing the artwork to be the focus. The other approach is to purchase works that blend well with your interior palette, combining colours, shapes, forms and styles that are completely in keeping with your interior. This ensures a harmonious space where the artwork is a team player rather than the star. Either way works – it really comes down to personal preference and how avid an art collector you are. As a decorator, I can't help but be attracted to art that fits my home's colour scheme. Right now, I'm into artwork with ethereal themes and a palette of green and blue. I just can't help myself!

Don't be afraid to live with bare walls while you build your art collection. Wait until you have a number of beautiful pieces that fill your heart with joy. All good interiors take time to evolve – and this applies to the decoration for your walls.

Hanging your artwork is as important a step as buying it, and scale is the most important box to tick when you're finding a wall for your art. For your art to truly sing, it needs to be hung in a way that reflects both its scale and its content. An oversized canvas hung on a small wall does not make for a harmonious space, and nor does a tiny canvas on a large wall. When the scale is wrong, it doesn't matter how beautiful the painting is, the result won't feel right.

Grouping art in various combinations makes for an eclectic and interesting feature in your space. For the ultimate wonder wall, scatter canvases of varying size and genre on the one wall. Mix up the styles by including illustrations, paintings, decorative carvings and photographs. For a cohesive and harmonious wall, ensure that each piece has a common element, most likely colour or possibly subject. Hang a series of artworks in a row along a hallway or galley. Grouping artworks in odd numbers seems to ensure a kind of balance. Stack art vertically if you have a small sliver of wall that could do with livening up. In this case, the frames should be similar, to ensure flow from top to bottom. If you have only two pieces, create interest on a wall by hanging them side by side, with one slightly higher than the other.

TIP: HANGING ARTWORK

To help you decide where and how to hang your art, cut out pieces of newspaper or brown paper the same size and stick them to the wall with masking tape, moving them around until you're sure their scale suits the space.

Don't be restrained by your overall decorating scheme when choosing artwork – instead, go for what you love. A quirky canvas can add pop in an otherwise sedate scheme.

Mirrors

Mirrors provide us not only with our own reflection, but also an alternative type of artwork to paintings or sculpture. Frames come in so many styles, from elaborately decorated to rough and rustic or modern and streamlined. A home filled with mirrors of various shapes, sizes and styles offers a window, a portal and a sneak peek into every corner of your room from every angle. As you saunter past a mirror, you can catch a framed glimpse of your space or beyond.

There are many ways to integrate mirrors into your home. A lovely approach is to group several on one wall, giving you a series of the same vignette. To add interest to the space, choose mirrors in various shapes. A mix of small and large round, oval, square or rectangular mirrors with varying frames, from aged and vintage to modern and streamlined, creates aesthetic interest. Alternatively, to create a modern feel, go for a series of mirrors in the same style of frame, in the same colour and material (say white or deep chocolate timber veneer) but in different widths to mix it up a little.

If you want a large mirror with a decorative frame, then stick to that one rather than having a few, to ensure it remains the focus in the room. A mirror in a confined space, such as a hallway or entrance area, ensuite bathroom or annexe, can add the illusion of space and the feeling that there's extra 'air' in your home. A mirror on a wall beyond a doorframe can add extra impact. In my old farmhouse, I have some arched doorways, relics from a 1980s renovation. To add impact but also to draw attention away from the arches (which feel a little daggy), I've placed a very large mirror with an elaborated carved off-white timber frame on the other side of the arch. It looks dramatic and downright beautiful in the space and does the job of drawing the eye away from the less attractive architectural elements of my home.

This is an important point – mirrors (and in fact all decorative elements in your home) are there not only to add beauty but also to highlight or conceal the best or worst architectural details. And so, put your pieces to work. You'll be surprised how effective they can be.

Mirrors aren't just for gazing in – they can also work as artwork, particularly if they have an ornate frame like this one.

Cushions

Cushions are like the icing on the cake, or the candy in the candy store — they're bright, colourful and easy to consume in vast quantities. Cushions are the most interchangeable element in your interior, and probably the least expensive — even if you go for a designer fabric and have them made — which gives you freedom to play around with colour, style and pattern (for more on choosing cushion fabrics, see page 134). This means you can, say, go for a bright and colourful palette in lazy linens for summer, then change to a warm and fuzzy winter palette in velvet, chenille and wool.

I encourage you to change and interchange, a little like you do with your bed linen, to ensure your space remains interesting and of the moment. To create a well-rounded aesthetic, invest in cushions of various shapes and sizes. Large, square, European-style cushions, measuring, say, 60 × 60 centimetres through to smaller scatter cushions measuring 20 × 20 centimetres are mainstay sizes for accessorising larger items such as sofas and armchairs. But don't be afraid to play around with the measurements, particularly if you're having cushions made to order. Rectangular cushions along the back of your sofa will give the space a streamlined feel. Bolster cushions add a little theatre, and are ideal on the inside of your sofa arms or at either end of a structured day bed. Circular cushions in all sizes layer beautifully with square cushions.

The key when arranging cushions is to mix shapes, sizes and styles rather than sticking to just one. A large European-style cushion layered with a smaller square cushion and then a circular cushion makes for an interesting sofa. Ditto an oversized rectangular back-cushion layered with smaller square cushions and one or two circular cushions. If you're thinking this sounds like a lot of cushions, you're right. Never under-cushion a piece of furniture, unless you're after a minimalist effect.

When pairing fabrics, begin with your largest pattern (say a big floral or geometric design) for your back cushion, then move through to smaller patterns (small floral, striped or geometric designs) as you move towards the front cushion. I call this approach 'stepping stones'. Beginning with the largest ensures certainty and a solid aesthetic root system.

Decorative elements, such as piping, fringes, braid and tassels can transform a mundane cushion and fabric into something a little more special. Go for detail in a colour that matches one element of the pattern and colour in your cushion. A simple block-colour cushion is given some oomph when piped in either a complementary colour or, for a harmonious effect, a tone of the base colour. A rough-textured fringe lends your cushion a natural, rustic air. A bright and shiny tassel offers a luxurious flavour. Ribbon trims work particularly well on old-style, rolled-arm sofas and armchairs rather than contemporary shapes, which require little adornment.

The key to successful cushioning lies in the mix of shapes, sizes and styles, and your choice of cushion insert. Go for feather inserts for pure comfort. Yes, they do need puffing up from time to time, but nothing beats their well-worn, well-loved appearance.

TIP: CUSHION STUFFING

Feathers are the only way to stuff a cushion, I say! They make for a cosy, tactile and downright comfy cushion, one that moves, one that feels, one that you never want to leave. The downside to feather-filled is (I can hear you saying it from here) they continually need to be fluffed. This is a drag, true, but worth it because they look and feel so good. If yours is a more formal space, one that requires a more upright look and feel, then consider foam stuffing, but I warn you, you'll never feel as cosy and comfy in the space. A mix of feather and filler offers a cushion that holds its shape but has a soft, relaxing feel. Alternative hypoallergenic fibres, such as corn fibre, are currently attracting attention. Off-the-shelf cushion inserts come in standard sizes – 20 ×× 20, 40 ×× 40 and 60 ×× 60 centimetres – but you can have inserts made to size, so speak to your upholsterer about your options. Cushions should always feel plump and full, so don't skimp by going for a lightweight insert.

Collections

Our collections are a little like a character map, reflecting our innermost self, so it's important to gather and display with thought and insight. What do you collect? Teacups? Glassware? Vases? Bottles? Antique wooden spoons?

My favourite thing to collect is ceramics. Everywhere I go in the world, I'll search high and low for local ceramic artists and buy a piece or two for my collection. I love ceramics – they're tactile and they've been made by hand with love and care. They're often beautifully coloured, and the purity of the glaze adds another exciting element, transporting me to a very happy place. Some pieces are more refined than others, which are well and truly handmade, but whatever their form, they tell a beautiful story of the place I've visited and of its people.

I tend to collect a lot of bits and pieces, but everything I collect is utilitarian – it has a purpose. Teacups and saucers are one favourite, notebooks another, as are perfume bottles, plates and cutlery. While every piece has a different form and purpose, there are certain similarities in everything I collect, probably because every piece appeals to my personal aesthetic.

If you go through your own collections, I bet you'll see a thread of continuity – perhaps a colour, form or style, or perhaps all three. Identifying this thread will help when you come to display your collection. If you haven't started collecting yet, you're in an ideal position – you can identify the common thread you're drawn to and stick to it as you collect. Let's say,

Your collections reveal your innermost self – the things that have meaning for you, and the path you've trodden – so it makes sense to display them with pride. Collections are best housed and displayed in vessels of all shapes, sizes and materials, such as timber bowls, glass jars and ceramic dishes.

for example, that your thread is the colour cream. It doesn't have to be more convoluted than that. And so, from this day forward, all your collections will somehow embody the colour cream, or a variation on cream. Steer yourself towards ceramics with a clotted-cream-coloured base, add to that a collection of antique spoons with cream-coloured bone handles and you've taken the first step towards building a collection. Don't be too rigid, though. You don't have to stick to one colour and your collections can be as varied and diverse as you are. Choosing a theme is simply a good beginning.

Once you've gathered a few bits and pieces, you need to think about how to display them. Collections look best when they're framed – in a display cabinet, a shadow box, a series of shelves or open cubbyholes. This holds the elements together, providing a solid structure within which they appear cohesive and connected. As a general rule, display your collections in odd numbers. Large, stand-alone pieces can be displayed on their own – don't crowd them with loads of other pieces. These include glassware such as vases or glass sculpture, oversized ceramic pieces such as vases and bowls, or porcelain figurines. Display mid-sized pieces in threes or fives and smaller pieces, such as shells, cutlery and vintage cotton reels, in another vessel – shells in a glass jar or dish, cutlery tied together with twine and placed on a rectangular dish, vintage cotton reels lying in a wooden bowl.

Flowers

Sometimes a room needs no more adornment than a simple vase filled with beautiful flowers. Flowers add aesthetic appeal to every space, whether it's a living room, kitchen, bathroom or bedroom, but they also add sensory appeal, particularly those with a strong and sweet scent.

Flower arrangements can be as simple or as complicated as you please. Flowers such as gardenias, jasmine and magnolias, especially when picked straight from the garden, look sweet and unstructured on their own in a small vase or a vintage bottle. Don't be too fussy with the arrangement of garden flowers – their appeal is their simplicity. These flowers aren't necessarily the focus in a room, but provide a secret vignette in a space.

Larger, more structured arrangements, on the other hand, work as a feature and focus point, so the aim is to wow. There are two ways to go with feature flowers – an oversized bunch of the same bloom (such as a vase filled to the brim with hydrangeas of one colour) will make a resounding statement, while a mixture of bold and bright flowers (such as orchids mixed with open peonies or open roses and cascading greenery) is an artistic approach. A mixed series of vases or bottles, each containing a single flower or flower head, such as lilacs, adds drama to a sideboard or dining table.

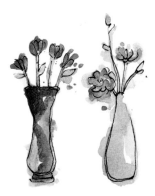

Avoid using florists' foam in the bottom of your vase — a vase filled with an unstructured arrangement is modern and organic. If your flowers need further support, placing them in a small vase or glass and then placing that in a larger vase will give them a more upright appearance. If structure is your thing, however, go for a more sculptured flower, such as a lily or rose, or a pod. For the best result, the key is to work with the flower rather than against it.

For a burst of excitement in a room, choose flowers in a complementary colour to your furnishings. For a cohesive space, choose flowers that are tonally in keeping with your scheme. A vase of all-white flowers, such as white lilies, lilac, roses or peonies, is always in fashion. Ensure that you have a range of vases on hand for your floral arrangements — and think outside the square when choosing vessel shapes and styles. Everything from a ceramic bowl to an old tin bucket works beautifully and adds an extra touch of personality.

Always resnip the stems of your flowers before you pop them into your vase. Fill the vase with fresh water and change it often to keep the flowers as fresh as possible.

Foliage

If a trip to the florist isn't on the agenda and there are no flowers in your garden, snip branches from the bushes in your garden instead. You'll often find me deep in the bushes around the farm, looking for interesting foliage or tree branches in varying shapes and colours both to decorate my home and to use when I'm styling photographic shoots. Literally stuffed into a vase, colourful foliage is sometimes all that's required to lift a table setting or lounge room. Favourite styles and colours of mine are rustic reds, oranges and deep greens, and the leaves of native flora such as wattle, bottlebrush, waratah and eucalyptus for their scent. For the most dramatic effect, keep them large, bountiful and cascading.

Flowers, foliage and fallen branches from the garden make a dramatic statement in this rustic dining room.

Pot plants

Indoor plants such as palms, ferns, cacti and succulents can all lift an interior. They literally add life to a space, offering us air to breathe. They're tactile, connect us with the outside world and, most importantly, bring nature indoors. A connection with nature is important for us as human beings, but not everyone can live close to nature. A home adorned with plants goes part of the way to creating our own little piece of nature indoors.

It's important to think about plants when you're drawing up the plans for your interior space – they're as important an element as your sofa or dining table. Plants soften the architectural edges in your home, providing organic shapes and gentle shadows that help add another dimension to your interior and make living in the space easier and happier.

The key when choosing plants is research. First up, you need to look at how your space functions and the amount of light it receives, as these will both greatly influence whether a plant will survive. Next, look at how large the plants will grow, to ensure their scale at full growth will match your space. Then, and most importantly, consider how much care the plant requires to keep it healthy and alive. Unless these requirements fit into your lifestyle, your beautiful green and lush interior could quickly turn brown and dry.

You also need to consider whether the plants will blend well with your overall aesthetic scheme. If yours is an interior filled with rustic tones and textured fabrics, then native plants in muted colours will blend perfectly. If yours is an interior made up of luscious colours and fabrics, then the femininity of cascading palms standing in every corner is ideal. This is the case in my house, which is filled with peacock-coloured velvets and deep chocolate Bentwood chairs reminiscent of the classic 1920s interiors seen in movies like *The Great Gatsby*. Once you've done all your research, buy your plants.

Plants in various sizes and shapes can round out every corner of your space. Try filling 'dead' corners with large plants, and empty surfaces such as sideboards and credenzas with small plants. Layer medium-sized plants around your large pots or dedicate a corner of a room to your own indoor greenhouse.

Finding great pots to display your plants can sometimes be trickier than sourcing the plant. In my experience, the key is to spend loads of time looking. This could be a lifetime adventure, particularly if you're trying to source pots that fit perfectly with your overall decorative theme – which of course you are! The last thing you need is to buy a boring pot simply to fill an empty corner. And while terracotta pots, particularly the old rustic kind, can be beautiful in their own right, their colour and style don't work in every space.

Plants add a living dimension to your interior scheme. Use shapes and forms that complement your interior style. Here, agaves, with their simple shape and form, are perfectly paired with utilitarian decorative elements.

And so, how to approach your pot searches? Bear in mind that the pot has as much aesthetic interest in a room as every other feature in it, so to begin, decide on a base colour to look for. In my home, all the walls and many of my built-ins, such as my bookshelf and TV cabinet, are white – and so it makes sense to extend the white theme through to the pots. Of course, white is an easy option, as so many white pots in varying sizes are available. On my travels, I've also come across some pots that fit nicely with my peacock-coloured sofa – and so, white and peacock have formed the base of my pot palette. White will be too stark and cold, however, if your interior is of a warmer, cosier palette. In this case, consider terracotta, charcoal or pots glazed in a colour that fits with your scheme. If these are too dark, go for a stone pot in a taupe or warm off-white, which will lift an otherwise muted palette.

Most exciting are pot finds that are completely out of the mould – and for this you'll need to pop on your walking shoes and scour the local markets, op shops and the side of the road on throw-out days. One truly unique pot will bring the basic shape and style of your other pots to life.

Books

A simple way to add interest to a space is to display your book collection. I'm an avid book collector – and have piles and piles of art and interiors books strategically placed in bookshelves and cubbyholes or as decoration on sideboards and my old-fashioned Le Corbusier settee. Books are just so beautiful. The love, the labour, the time that has gone into not only the writing but also the design of the book are worthy of display. And a room filled with a good dose of books makes an interesting space to hang out in.

When my mother, who lives in the city, comes to stay at the farm, she spends days and days perusing my ever-growing collection of books. They provide us with hours of relaxation and interest. Books tell you what interests a person, what their passions are, what their life focus is. If you were to read me through my books, you'd see very quickly that I've dedicated my life to all things home – numerous interior design and cookery books line every surface, with a good dose of gardening books and a smattering of health, healing and happiness books. On occasion I'll break out into a new area of interest, but by and large I'm a lover of all things homey and gorgeous.

Of course, I'm not the only person in our house – and so we also have a mix of travel and geography books reflecting my hubby's interest in the world beyond our front doorstep, an immeasurable amount of *Doctor Who* paraphernalia (our son Joe's interest) and books on fashion (our daughter Inez's passion). When I'm styling a house for a magazine, I love nothing more than checking out the bookshelves, as this gives me a great insight into who lives in the space.

If books are part of your decorating armoury, there are only a couple of guidelines to ensuring they look neat and tidy and are easy to access. The simplest and most aesthetic approach is to file them in blocks of colour — using the spines as your colour guide. I love nothing more than a bookshelf approached in this manner — it offers a kaleidoscope of colour at every glance. If you need to use your books on a regular basis and require more than just aesthetic order, then file your books in sections of subject matter, and even alphabetically within each subject. While the bookshelf will appear a little messier on the aesthetic front, it will help you find what you need. Books in vertical stacks look neat and tidy, but can be a pain to get out if you need to look at them often. If you're dealing with an oversized bookshelf or oversized books and would like to add some aesthetic interest, then mix things up with some books in piles and others filed horizontally. Add a few ornaments around the books for good measure, and you have a jumbo-sized and ultra-interactive artwork on your wall — one that moves and changes as you do.

Floor rugs

Floor rugs are an integral component in any decorating scheme — they not only add a layer of comfort underfoot, but offer aesthetic interest in a room. Some floor rugs can even act as one of the artworks in your space. The style and design of floor rug you choose very much depends on the decorative choices you've already made.

For balance and harmony, it's important to carry the decorative sensibility all the way through to the floor. A rustic woollen kilim rug with random organic patterning is a great option if your interior includes rustic and textured elements, but not so great for a high-end glamorous interior that relies on luxurious decorative elements such as silk and velvet. A designer rug in bold geometric shapes and cool Scandinavian colours works well in a streamlined interior with little in the way of fussy decorative adornment. It's not a good idea to mix design sensibilities, so be sure to incorporate your rug into your entire decorative scheme. These are the most common rug styles you'll encounter:

KILIM (KELIM)   Originating in such countries as Iran, Turkey and Afghanistan, kilims are tribal, flat-weave, textured, highly patterned and rustic. They're a popular choice, particularly if yours is a relaxed interior with loads of textured fabrics and simple organic patterns and shapes. Although more and more these days are synthetically dyed to achieve a longer lasting colour, they're often made from naturally dyed wools and thus fit into a muted and subdued colour palette. Kilim rugs work well with neutral and warm-toned upholstery and furnishings.

A decorative rug can add drama to a space through the combination of colour, pattern and size. Rugs are an artwork, so treat a rug as the focus in the room and make your other decorative choices accordingly.

PERSIAN Hand-knotted with a flat pile, Persian rugs are soft underfoot and comfortable, as well as highly decorative. Often more luxurious, more refined and less textured than kilims, Persian rugs are stylish and work beautifully in a home filled to the brim with antique furniture (either farmhouse or stately) and indulgent fabrics such as velvet, silk and fine linen.

MODERN A multitude of modern designer rugs is available for your decorating pleasure. A designer rug is a statement piece, often boldly patterned and coloured – an artwork for your floor. A richly patterned rug becomes the focus in a room and so works well with an interior scheme that's based around block colour, where the furnishings don't compete with the rug. To ensure continuity and flow in the space, choose a rug with one or two colours from your general colour scheme. Patchwork rugs, while modern, add a rustic, handmade flavour to a space.

SISAL, COIR, SEAGRASS AND PAPER Simple, textured and natural, these floor rugs provide a bit of interest to the floor without overwhelming the interior scheme. Being neutral in nature and colour, they play more of a supporting role in a room and are more about texture. Perfectly paired with a timber, concrete or tiled floor, they provide a relaxed and laid-back flavour to a space and work well with all interior styles, from city pad to country house and beach shack. Well priced and easy to care for, they're the ideal no-fuss rugs.

Throw rugs

Adding another layer of comfort, texture and colour to a space, throw rugs are a must in a home, particularly if you spend hours on the sofa reading or watching movies (like me and my family!). The right throw rug can add to the feeling of calm and relaxation, and so is an important component that should be thought about carefully. Texture and size are the key elements to consider here – could there be anything more vexing than curling up on the sofa, cup of tea in hand, only to find that what you thought was a luxurious and divine throw rug in fact leaves you well and truly itching and scratching? Try soft and lovely cashmere, which won't offend your skin. While not particularly high-end, an oversized polar fleece throw rug is the bee's knees in terms of comfort. Just be sure to choose one in a colour that blends into your interior scheme.

For me, however, the ideal throw rug combines beauty and comfort in the form of a quilt – filled with lightweight feather and down and covered in a stylish fabric, it adds to the whole interior scheme rather than detracts from it.

Bric-a-brac

It's the little bits and pieces, the smaller collections of things, that lend personality and depth to an interior. If you're a bric-a-brac collector, you'll know exactly what I'm talking about. Ceramic bowls and glass jars filled with vintage cotton reels and buttons then placed just so on shelves and surfaces; postcards and photographs on the pin board; piles of magazines in a stylish modern magazine rack; pictures in ramshackle frames; baskets; candles; teacups piled high; plates precisely configured on the wall; children's paintings on the refrigerator or their clay creations taking pride of place on the mantelpiece – these are a few of my favourite things that bring my space to life. They remind me, every day, of my life: where I've been and where I'm going. They offer me a glimpse of times past – of days spent with my family, of happy holiday memories. They make me smile.

While a home filled with bric-a-brac can require extra dusting (!) – the effort is worth it if you're surrounded by the things you love. If you'd like a uniform space, collect your bric-a-brac with your interior style in mind. If yours is a modern and streamlined interior, seek bric-a-brac that reflects these design sensibilities, or display your smaller, more disparate pieces in a streamlined, modern larger piece. If yours is an earthy and textured environment, look to bric-a-brac that reflects this sense of style, such as parched vintage papers or worn timbers such as driftwood. If a high-gloss and glamorous interior is more your speed, go after shiny jewels such as glassware and crystals – everything from simple drinking goblets to elaborate crystal vases and decanters.

Whatever your bric-a-brac heaven, it needs to be ordered and easily accessible if it's to function well in your space and not overwhelm you.

Display your bric-a-brac in a cabinet designed to show your collections in the best possible light. This vintage mirrored cabinet makes a lovely backdrop to the delicate shell-encrusted vessels that line its shelves.

LAYER TEN

Styling it all together

The power of styling

And so, here we are – almost at the end of our decorating journey together. If you've now implemented layers one to nine, you should be living in a space you love – a thoughtful interior, one that represents who you are, what you love and how you like to live. If you're not quite there yet, you're no doubt well and truly on your way, so don't worry – unless you're a professional decorator, you're free to take your time, allowing your interior to evolve and grow with your knowledge and confidence. After all, there's no rush. Decorating your home could take you a lifetime, and what an incredibly creative life's work that would be, I say.

To top off all the hard work you've done so far there's one final step. And the good news is it's the best part of all – styling together all your bits and pieces. How you present the things in your house goes a long way towards the overall effect you can create, so this is the layer in the process that gives your home its extra kick. The styling rules I'm going to tell you here can be applied to any space, whether it's been fully decorated or is in the process of being decorated or whether decorating your house is but a distant dream for you right now. Some of the women who come along to my workshops aren't in a position to make massive inroads into the decoration of their home. They may be renting, for example, and don't want to invest a fortune in furniture and upholstery that won't be easy to integrate into later rental places. Or perhaps their funds won't extend to a brand-new interior design scheme that flows from room to room.

Luckily, when it comes to styling, it doesn't matter whether your home is old or new or whether you have a fully decorated space. Some thoughtful rearranging can completely change the look and, more importantly, the feel of your interior. Styling can reinvigorate your space. It can positively change the energy around you and turn what you thought was old and boring into new and exciting.

You'll often find me rearranging the things in my home – nothing, from the largest items of furniture to the smallest details, is immune to a little rearranging at times, often in an off-the-cuff way, late at night, when everyone's in bed and my mind is clearest! And so, this section is dedicated to a few hard and fast rules to style by, straight out of my Styling 101 workshop for budding stylists. Although the principles I teach there are ultimately designed for photographic styling work, the same rules apply to creating vignettes in your home.

Through the viewfinder

Sometimes the most insightful way to see how your home looks is through the viewfinder. I find that when you put a framework around a space, as would a camera on a photo shoot, you can better see the elements in your room and their relationship to each other. I like to apply this same principle to a home and – just as we would on a shoot – it's a good idea to snap away at your space to see exactly what's going on. Take a mixture of large room shots – so that you can see how the larger items of furniture are working together – combined with some smaller vignette photos, such as of your collections and corner arrangements. Shoot, shoot, shoot. One picture of the space is never enough.

Take loads of different snapshots from every angle and then edit your shots. A good idea is to take pictures from the angles you usually see your space – upon entering the room, sitting on the sofa, from your bed and walking from space to space. Don't be too hard on yourself if your pictures don't quite look up to scratch first off – shooting like a professional takes time and practice. And like decorating, the skill of photographing your space is one that evolves.

Once you've taken a series of pictures, download them onto your computer and see how they're looking. Be critical, and try to detach yourself emotionally from the space. How's the scale looking? Are your furniture items relating well to each other? Is there balance in the room? What would you change to fill out the frame a little better? Think like a stylist and be tough if you need to be. In my experience as a stylist in other people's homes, I've learnt that my job is less about bringing things into a shot and more about taking things out of it. You might find that this is the case with your space, too. Be tough – you'll reap the benefit from a space that's balanced and in harmony.

An insightful way to evaluate whether your furnishings and decorations are working together is to photograph your room from various angles, as a photographer would for an interiors magazine. You'll soon see if things need to be rearranged to achieve a more coherent space.

Creating a vignette

A vignette is a smaller scene, a detail within the larger scene or room. Vignettes are the glue in a space and, as they're made up of collections and beautiful shapes and forms, offer the most personality and character. You'd create a vignette within a glass-fronted cabinet, for example, or on a mantelpiece, a sideboard or the centre of a large dining table. Vignettes bring excitement and interest to a room, telling a story and drawing people in. It's important to arrange your vignettes well and in proportion for two reasons: first because you want your room to appear completely balanced and in harmony, and secondly because you want to put your things together in the most natural and gorgeous way, ensuring that the essence of each piece is respected and given its due time to shine.

There are a few important rules for creating a vignette:

1   **THINK IN ODD NUMBERS**   If you have one large and ever so exquisite piece that needs a stage all to itself – such as a large glass sculpture, an oversized ceramic bowl or a special lamp – then display it on its own. Make sure you get the scale right – it really needs to take up room on the surface and not be overcrowded. If you have a range of beautiful but smaller pieces that vary enough in height and scale to be interesting, but not so much that one piece is dwarfed by the others, move up to threes (and then fives). Use your critical eye to adjust the arrangement – and then take a picture (see page 190). It will be immediately obvious if the pieces have a happy relationship. If they don't, remove the odd one out and replace it with another, then take another shot and repeat until all is well.

2   **MIX OR MATCH**   Either mix up your styles and textures to ensure that your vignette remains interesting, or keep your collection to just one colour or textural theme. A glass cabinet filled with green milk glass in various shapes and sizes – jugs, goblets, bowls, and so on – is easy to look at, as the uniformity of colour and style ensures cohesion and harmony. If you're mixing styles, the pieces need a common thread – an element of colour, texture or form that holds the collection together. Once you've created your vignette, throw in an odd piece for good measure – this will keep your vignette alive and well and truly on its toes.

3   **USE THE 'STEP-DOWN' RULE**   When choosing sizes to group together, think of putting one high piece at the back, one medium piece to the side and one smaller piece at the front, with a small step down in size from one piece to the next. This rule applies to any vignette, large or small. In the corner of a room, for example, have the floor lamp at the back, the armchair in the middle and the ottoman or side table at the front and just off to the side. Always step each piece down a notch while making sure each has a connection to the other – a very high floor lamp behind a very squat armchair, for example, does not a happy marriage make! Always look, see and style.

4   **LAYER UPON LAYER**   Take the layered look one step further by filling vessels with smaller curios. Vintage cotton reels in a coloured glass bowl add another dimension to the bowl. Your seashell collection in a clear glass cylinder brings the glass vessel to life. Vintage binoculars resting atop a pile of antique books draws the eye to your vignette. A cluster of antique perfume bottles sitting in a circular rattan tray gives purpose to the tray. An old-fashioned fan lying on the lid of an Indian bone-inlaid jewellery box makes what's inside the box even more interesting. Layer cushions and throw rugs over larger items of furniture to soften their edges and make the space appear more homely and liveable. Remember the rule of less is more, however, and always take one or two pieces away from the scene to ensure you haven't overdone the room.

5   **PRACTISE, PRACTISE, PRACTISE**   When it comes to creating vignettes, practice is the most important thing and the only way you'll become adept at creating beautiful and thoughtful vignettes. Some people do have a natural gift for such things, it's true, but at the end of the day, with a little dedication and practice, we all have it in us to create a worthy scene. And so dedicate yourself to it. Play, practise and photograph your endeavours. If you're the type, fill an inspiration book with what you've created and discovered. This is a wonderful way to see your talent evolve. And remember, styling your home is meant to be fun, so please enjoy yourself! It's the stuff of dreams, after all.

It's all in the details. To create small vignettes that work, use the odd-number rule. Here, the three main elements provide balance on the cabinet top, while the picture on the wall and the peacock feather add height and interest above them.

Conclusion: You're home

What fun we've had and what a joyful journey it's been. I do so love the art of decorating a home! I've said it before but I must say it again, the way you decorate your home can have a huge effect on how you feel about your life. When we decorate our home thoughtfully and with love (not necessarily with large funds), we're creating a space we love living in, a home with meaning, a house that feels comfortable, a place to feel at peace with ourselves. And what a gift this is, having a retreat within which we can unwind, where we can peel back the layers and be exactly who we are. If you look at it this way, creating a space that supports this powerful process is a must, not just for our aesthetic pleasure but also for our spiritual pleasure. Now you have the tools to create this for yourself and the framework to kick-start the journey.

My advice is to keep this book close as you begin down the decorating road – you'll need to refer to it often to clarify and support your thoughts and ideas. Once you get the knack of it all, however, you'll need to refer to it less and less, except to be inspired by the beautiful pictures, of course! Like all elements of creativity, decorating a home is an ever-evolving pursuit and never really ends, because as you grow and change so will your interior. In this way, the process is organic, so be sure to go with the flow. Play, tinker, move, change and grow. Allow your space to evolve as your skill builds and your life transforms. Most of all, be sure to have fun with it – decorating should always be a joy, so try not to get bogged down.

I wish you well in your decorating journey. Be bold, be creative, be you and enjoy the decorating ride. It will make you smile – I promise!

Suppliers

While researching great products makes up part of the decorating equation, creating a solid, trusting relationship with your suppliers is just as important, if not more so. Your suppliers are your support in the creation of an extraordinary interior, so it's important to foster your relationships with great care and respect. If you're a professional decorator, speak to your suppliers about opening trade accounts, which will enable you to source and buy products at trade prices. Each supplier will have specific sales terms and conditions, so be sure to find out what they are before you order. Your supplier will be able to give you an estimate of the recommended retail price of each product, as a guideline to invoicing your client. Trade prices can vary anywhere from 10–50 per cent of the retail price.

Fabric

BIRD TEXTILES birdtextile.com.au
Organic fabrics in original patterns; a favourite for everything from tabletop supplies to cushions and lampshades.

SOUTH PACIFIC FABRICS
southpacificfabrics.com
I love South Pacific for many reasons but mostly because they supply the lovely Kenzo fabrics, which have played the starring role in a number of interiors I've designed over the years.

RADFORD FURNISHINGS
radfordfurnishings.com
As a lover of colour, I'm always looking to Designers Guild for their bright and bold fabrics and Matisse-inspired patterns. Pure sophistication, William Yeoward's fabrics add an upper-crust finish to even the most relaxed setting.

UNIQUE FABRICS uniquefabrics.com
A comprehensive cross-section of fabrics; everything from linens in muted tones to bold patterns in the brightest palette. Try Andrew Martin for funky rock-star fabrics in over-the-top Brit-inspired patterns – think the Beatles and the Union Jack.

WESTBURY TEXTILES
westburytextiles.com
Westbury is my first stop when looking for natural-fibre fabrics, such as cottons and linens, in a barely-there neutral palette.

NO CHINTZ nochintz.com
Off-the-roll fabrics in a range of colours and patterns – everything from candy stripes to florals.

ICI ET LÀ icietla.com.au
Ici et Là stripes are a mainstay for many of my interiors. I particular love their outdoor stripes, which are ideal for sun lounges and over-sized cushions.

MOKUM TEXTILES
mokumtextiles.com
Beautifully appointed fabrics in fashionable ranges – made to last the distance.

CLOTH FABRIC clothfabric.com
Contemporary and natural textiles, inspired by nature and printed onto hemp and linen, define this offbeat range.

AMY BUTLER amybutlerdesign.com
Bright clashing colours in patterns reminiscent of days long gone – Amy Butler fabrics are an infusion of fun and fashion.

SIX HANDS sixhands.com.au
Cutting-edge is the best way to describe this company of young and fashion-forward designers.

THIBAUT–BOYAC boyac.com.au
Thibaut's classic French-inspired designs add majesty and grandeur to a room.

JOHN ROBSHAW TEXTILES
johnrobshaw.com
A contemporary take on classic Indian patterning, these fabrics are modern and of the moment.

KATHRYN M. IRELAND
kathrynireland.com
Muted tones, repetitive patterning and Spanish-esque designs with a modern twist from the effervescent Kathryn Ireland.

WARWICK FABRICS warwick.com.au
A reliable range of fabrics at prices that make decorating accessible to all.

ANNE LEON anneleon.com
Inspired-by-nature patterning in warm, muted earth tones.

KELANI FABRIC OBSESSION
kelanifabric.com.au
Modern fabrics with a vintage twist.

MARIMEKKO marimekko.com
Colourful Finnish fabrics in bold prints.

Wallpaper

FERM LIVING fermliving.com.au
Pared-back Danish design inspired by the stillness of nature.

JOCELYN WARNER
jocelynwarner.com
Delicate forms in sumptuous colour ways define this fashionable range of wallpapers.

ELLI POPP ellipopp.com
Colourful, funky, clever. Elli Popp, you're a winner!

THE SELVEDGE GROUP
theselvedgegroup.com.au
Deep, dark, brooding and highly designed, this expansive range of wallpapers will add depth to a space.

**FLORENCE BROADHURST –
SIGNATURE PRINTS**
signatureprints.com.au
Folly and 1960s style define all things Florence Broadhurst. Her designs are as modern today as when they were originally created.

**OSBORNE & LITTLE – SENECA
TEXTILES** senecatextiles.com.au
Classic, colourful, witty and upbeat, Osborne & Little wallpapers make a long-lasting but easy-to-live-with impact.

RADFORD FURNISHINGS
radfordfurnishings.com
Loose and organic combined with bright and cheerful, Designers Guild wallpapers define a way of living for laid-back moderns. Cole & Son wallpapers have stood the test of time, each an artwork in its own right. Palm Leaves is a favourite of mine.

ABIGAIL EDWARDS – MUROBOND
murobond.com.au
Hand-drawn and ever so quirky, these wallpapers are created using hand-mixed colours in non-toxic water-based inks.

PUBLISHER TEXTILES
publishertextiles.com.au
A showcase of avant-garde hand-printed fabrics and wallpapers in deep, dark, brooding tones.

Paint

MUROBOND murobond.com.au
These textured paints in a comprehensive range of fashion colours are a favourite for all painting jobs, large or small.

PORTER'S PAINTS porters.com.au
If you're thinking lime wash and fresco, Porter's Paints is your brand.

ECOLOUR ecolour.com.au
These non-toxic paints come in any colour, with no volatile organic compounds (VOCs).

DULUX dulux.com.au
Hard-wearing and in an extensive range of colours, Dulux paints are easy to use and last the distance.

Bed linen

SHANNON FRICKE BED LINEN
shannonfrickebedlinen.com
My bed linen is free range – pick and choose to create an individual bedding look.

LAZYBONES lazybones.com.au
Luscious, feminine and even downright girly, Lazybones is a bed-linen mainstay and a firm favourite among the fashion set.

CASTLE castleandthings.com.au
Simple, elegant and of the moment.

DWELL STUDIO dwellstudio.com
This range in notice-me patterns is a design heavyweight.

MATTEO matteohome.com
Loose, careful and fanciful – ideal if you're after a gentle 'whisper' of design on the bed.

SOCIETY societylimonta.com
Soft, muted colours in fluid, textured fabrics; Society is the matriarch of beautiful bedding.

Bedheads

BEDNEST bednest.com.au

HEATHERLY DESIGN
heatherlydesign.com.au

Rugs

ARMADILLO & CO
armadilloandco.com
Rough and highly textured, these rugs add an element of nature to your floor.

MILTON CATER ORIENTAL CARPETS
orientalcarpets.com.au
With luscious patterns reminiscent of a bygone era, Milton Cater rugs are the real deal if old-world kilim (kelim) and Persian rugs are for you.

DESIGNER RUGS
designerrugs.com.au
Modern and highly designed – look to the collaborations with well-known Australian designers for an original twist.

MOKUM TEXTILES
mokumtextiles.com
Beautifully appointed, well-made designer rugs in fluid patterns and sophisticated colour palettes.

THE RUG COMPANY
therugcompany.info
These are the most coveted rugs of all, the rock stars of flooring.

LOOM loomrugs.com.au
A contemporary take on traditional designs; the patchwork rugs are a firm favourite.

Lighting

PIERRE AND CHARLOTTE
pierreandcharlotte.com
These handcrafted lights are designed and made in Melbourne. The Big Tree Light standing lamp is simply beautiful.

SPENCE & LYDA
spenceandlyda.com.au
For George Nelson Bubble Lamps.

ECC LIGHTING & FURNITURE
ecc.com.au
The best of the best in European lighting.

Furniture

COTSWOLD FURNITURE
cotswoldfurniture.com.au
I've been using the legendary Vincent Sheppard loom range for years now. The Butterfly Lounge Chair straddles the line between contemporary and traditional.

ROBERT PLUMB
robertplumb.com.au
Robert Plumb outdoor furniture embodies classic design with a twist.

THONET thonet.com.au
Forever Thonet! Think elegant bentwood café chairs, sturdy Tolix stools and outdoor furniture.

JARDAN jardan.com.au
Sleek designs made to last the distance; Jardan furniture offers modernity with a softer edge.

BLACK & SPIRO
blackandspiro.com.au
Classic Hollywood regency-inspired furniture upholstered in extrovert fabrics in a style unique to Anna Spiro.

MARK TUCKEY marktuckey.com.au
This company specialises in the design and creation of solid timber furniture, predominantly in new and recycled Australian timbers.

SPENCE & LYDA
spenceandlyda.com.au
Designer furniture, textiles and homewares.

SPACE FURNITURE
spacefurniture.com.au
The cream of the crop in designer furniture, with brands like B&B Italia and Kartell. Look out for the Canasta range by Patricia Urquiola.

BEACHWOOD
content.beachwood.com.au
Chunky lime-washed beach-style furniture at its finest.

LAURA ASHLEY laura-ashley.com.au
Turn to their classically designed sofas and armchairs if rolled legs and tufting are your style.

HOUSE OF ORANGE
house-of-orange.com.au
Unique designs with a northern European aesthetic; this range of outdoor furniture is both functional and beautiful.

KOSKELA koskela.com.au
Produces Australian-made furniture, in particular using recycled timbers, in a range of off-the-floor and customised designs.

HOME FURNITURE ON CONSIGNMENT hfoc.com.au
A large range of pre-loved designer and contemporary pieces showcased in a 1100 square metre emporium of beauty!

FY2K fy2k.com.au
If the Richard Schultz Petal Table is a favourite, this is where you'll find it.

DAVID MET NICOLE
davidmetnicole.com
An eclectic range of original and sourced items — a beautiful mix of old and new.

DOUG UP ON BOURKE
douguponbourke.com.au
A large source of industrial, commercial and rustic antiques and hardcore collectables, situated in the middle of Sydney.

GREAT DANE
greatdanefurniture.com
The name says it all — yes, this is where you'll find the loveliest range of Danish and Scandinavian designed furniture.

PLANET planetfurniture.com.au
Beautifully crafted Australian-sourced furniture and homewares.

Accessories

JONATHAN ADLER
jonathanadler.com
Fun and funky with abounding humour, Jonathan Adler pottery and accessories will lighten up even the most sombre of interiors.

RACHEL ASHWELL'S SHABBY CHIC
shabbychic.com
Light and whimsical with a feminine edge.

BLUE CARAVAN bluecaravan.net
A one-stop shopping mecca for all things fair-trade and handmade.

OLDYARNS oldyarns.com.au
Beautiful, old-world linens repurposed into everything from cushions to tea-cosies.

KANIMBLA CLAY
kanimblaclay.blogspot.com
Delicate handmade ceramics inspired by nature and the Kanimbla Valley.

MISS ISA bluecaravan.net
Recycled-paper gifts — think rosettes and garlands.

DINOSAUR DESIGNS
dinosaurdesigns.com.au
Resin at its best, in translucent colours and organic forms.

PALACE DECOR AND DESIGN
palacemirrors.com.au
These beautiful new mirrors have the old-world patina of antique mirrors. Check out their beautifully chosen range of vintage furniture and accessories, too.

RUBY STAR TRADERS   rubystar.com
This decorating stalwart is a one-stop heavenly shop for imported Indian textiles, furniture and homewares.

BRAUERBIRDS   brauerbirds.com.au
A bowerbird collection of beautiful furniture, homewares and lighting.

ISLAND LUXE   islandluxe.com.au
Need an escape? Then an afternoon on Island Luxe with their tranquillity-inspired homewares and accessories will do the trick.

BLOOMINGVILLE   bloomingville.dk
Mix-and-match accessories with a cool Nordic twist.

FENTON & FENTON
fentonandfenton.com.au
Bright colour and bold eclectic patterning sets this Melbourne store apart from the rest.

PURE AND GENERAL
pureandgeneral.com
Curated with a deft hand and a wanderer's heart. Unique and eclectic homewares designed by artists, artisans and architects.

COTTON LOVE   cottonlove.com.au
Belgian-influenced homewares with a cool, laid-back edge.

ORSON & BLAKE
orsonandblake.com.au
This Sydney stalwart combines a heady mix of sophistication with masculine charm.

THE WHITE SHED
thewhiteshed.com.au
Beautifully chosen French-inspired homewares.

THE DHARMA DOOR
thedharmadoor.com.au
A leading source for contemporary, fair-trade and sustainable homewares.

ETSY   etsy.com
All things vintage and handmade.

NV NEW VINTAGE   nvnewvintage.com
A collection of well-selected vintage gems.

ART PIECE GALLERY
australianart.artpiecegallery.com.au
An extensive range of artist-created paintings, sculpture and ceramics.

THE BROWN TRADING CO.
thebrowntradingco.com.au
Colourful linens and cushions with a modern take on Indian-inspired patterning.

FUNKIS   funkis.com
Clean-lined Swedish form in everything from lighting to tabletop.

STRANGETRADER   strangetrader.com
A well-edited mix of contemporary and found homewares sourced in such faraway places as Turkey, Greece and Paris.

TABLE TONIC   tabletonic.com.au
Colourful and fun, with a solid range of homewares favourites.

THE SOCIETY INC
thesocietyinc.com.au
Heaven for the bowerbird – look to the range of pieces inspired by hardware and bric-a-brac.

MEGAN PARK   meganpark.co.uk
Luscious, decadent, simply beautiful cushions in original one-off designs.

ABC CARPET & HOME   abchome.com
Open in Manhattan since 1897, this is 10 floors of retail nirvana, stocking everything from one-off textiles to bedding and lighting.

TERRAIN AT STYERS
shopterrain.com
Organic and earthy homewares with a gardening bent.

AUNTY COOKIE   auntycookie.com
Funky, graphic cushions, fabrics and wallpapers.

HEAVEN IN EARTH
heaveninearth.com.au
Gardening heaven! Dress the outside as you do the inside with this stylish range of gardening accessories.

PAPER BOAT PRESS
paperboatpress.com
Thoughtfully created ceramic lovelies.

AURORA DESIGN STUDIO
auroradesignstudio.com.au
A clever mix of organic, handmade pieces and firm design favourites.

WAX JAMBU EMPORIUM
waxjambu.com.au
Indian-inspired homewares, a huge collection of interior-design books and the sweetest-smelling candles.

OBJECT GALLERY   object.com.au
Stunning Australian arts and crafts.

RED GINGER ASIAN FOOD & HOME
(02) 6680 9779
Stepping into Red Ginger is like stepping into an Asian market – and a beautiful and funky one at that.

IZZI & POPO   izziandpopo.com.au
Importers of European antiques – breadboards, garden chairs, tables, china, Murano glassware.

WHITE & WANDER
whiteandwander.com.au
Whimsical is the word for this lovely collection of new and found objects.

BECKER MINTY   beckerminty.com
A sophisticated collection of art and ornaments.

BOUNTIFUL   bountifulhome.com
This Santa Monica favourite is a vintage bowerbird's paradise. I particularly love the extensive range of cake stands.

Tabletop

JASPER CONRAN FOR WEDGWOOD
waterfordwedgwood.com.au
Hail Jasper! After all, he brought us the Wedgwood Chinoiserie range.

DONNA HAY FOR ROYAL DOULTON
donnahay.com.au
A must-have range of all-whites for the table.

FREE RANGE BY SHANNON FRICKE
shannonfricke.com
One-of-a-kind homewares designed for the individual in you.

MUD AUSTRALIA   mudaustralia.com
The finest ceramics in candy-store colours.

LUCY VANSTONE
vanstoneceramic.squarespace.com
Her crackle bowls are a favourite.

ELEPHANT CERAMICS
elephantceramics.com
Lovely, lovely, lovely – you'll fall in love with the blues and greens.

BISON AUSTRALIA   **bisonhome.com**
Country ceramics in delicate colour ways.

Storage

FIONA KATE   **fionakate.com.au**
The Postie is a favourite.

KIKKI.K   **kikki-k.com**
No excuses not to be organised after a trip to kikki.K.

HOWARDS STORAGE WORLD
hsw.com.au
For the big stuff, large well-made plastic storage bins in particular.

Bric-a-brac

HEATH'S OLD WARES
heathsoldwares.com.au
Ross and Eva Heath know their old wares like nobody else.

COUNTRY HOUSE ANTIQUES
countryhouseantiques.com.au
'Antiques made daily' is their motto! Beautifully repurposed country-inspired pieces.

THE NEW COLLECTOR
thenewcollector.blogspot.com
For the serious collector who likes their antiques with an industrial edge.

THE SOCIETY INC
thesocietyinc.com.au
Extensively sourced bric-a-bric with a stylist's eye for detail.

SECOND HAND ROSE   **(02) 6685 0120**
Repurposed vintage furniture and linens.

CLEM'S CARGO   **(02) 6685 1213**
Old wares in need of some tender loving care.

RESOULD   **resould.wordpress.com**
1950s, 1960s and 1970s pieces in mint condition.

RED NED'S SALVAGE & SECONDHAND
rednedssecondhand.com.au
Everything from second-hand kitchens to doors and windows in need of a loving home.

Tiles

JATANA INTERIORS
jatanainteriors.com.au
A colourful, exciting range of antique and reproduction tiles in patterns you'll love.

OLD WORLD TILES
oldworldtiles.com.au
Handmade tiles inspired by Spanish, Moroccan and Mexican styles.

SINTRA DESIGNS
sintraantiquetiles.com
Designs in Spanish, Dutch and Turkish styles. I love a decorative tile!

OLDE ENGLISH TILES AUSTRALIA
oldeenglishtiles.com.au
High-quality tiles for the heritage restorer in you.

AERIA COUNTRY FLOORS
aeria.com.au
The best of the best for your floor.

Pressed metal

PRESSED TIN PANELS
pressedtinpanels.com
I love pressed metal – on the walls, ceilings and built-ins.

WUNDERLITE   **wunderlite.com.au**
More pressed metal – in an extensive range of patterns.

Blogs

DAILY IMPRINT
dailyimprint.blogspot.com

DESIGN SPONGE
designsponge.com

ABSOLUTELY BEAUTIFUL THINGS
absolutelybeautifulthings.blogspot.com

DESIRE TO INSPIRE
desiretoinspire.net

DECOR8
decor8blog.com

APARTMENT THERAPY
apartmenttherapy.com

BEACH VINTAGE
beachvintage.blogspot.com

BELLAMUMMA
bellamumma.com

MADE BY GIRL
madebygirl.blogspot.com

BRABOURNE FARM
brabournefarm.blogspot.com

THE DESIGN FILES
thedesignfiles.net

HABITUALLY CHIC
habituallychic.blogspot.com

BROWN BUTTON
brownbutton.blogspot.com

MARLEY & LOCKYER
marleyandlockyer.blogspot.com

PIA JANE BIJKERK
blog.piajanebijkerk.com

A big thank you

The creation of a book is always a collaborative effort – the look and feel of every page is a collage of ideas and creative visions. And so, it is with respect that I say a big thank you to . . .

THE TEAM AT PENGUIN/LANTERN

Julie Gibbs – thank you for backing *How to Decorate* with gusto and for tending the process with grace. You run a creative hot pot at Lantern, and I'm very grateful to be a part of the action. Emily O'Neill – what a pleasure it has been to work with such an innovative art director! Thanks for your unwavering commitment to this project (and the relentless amount of hand-lettering) and your patience in the company of this rather opinionated author. Nicola Young – for your respect in the face of my never-ending ramblings and your gentle prodding to move me swiftly (but without pain) towards my very tight deadline.

THOSE WHO GRACIOUSLY OPENED THEIR DOORS

Thank you for allowing us into your homes and for permitting them to appear in this book. It is your decorating prowess that brings every page to life with colour, style and excitement: Ali Griffiths of Ali Griffiths Design; Melinda Trost; Helen and Mitchell English; Sam Wagner; Funkis; Anna Cayzer; Alexia Gnecchi Ruscone of Eclettica; Victoria Spring of NV Vintage; Kim Amos and Stephen Eakin of Atlantic Guesthouses, Byron Bay; Romaine and Dave (and Fawn Galli and Ashley Moyer of Fawn Galli Interiors) for giving me a lovely reason to travel to NYC and for hosting me so graciously; Sonya Marish of Jatana Interiors; Andrea Duff and Robert Schwamberg of Strangetrader and Byron View Farm; Valerie Hardy of Second Hand Rose, Brunswick Heads; Dee Hockley; Olivia and Adam Steel; Jan Chamberlain; and artist Hilary Herrmann.

GREAT STYLISTS

The work of some very talented stylists appears on these pages, and I thank them all with great admiration: Amanda Mahoney; Margot Braddon; Tami Christensen; and Anna Utzon.

THE INDEFATIGABLE PRUE RUSCOE

The beautiful work of this photographer extraordinaire appears on almost every page of this book. Thanks again for travelling to New York (and Newport, Rhode Island) on a whim, no less! This is our third book together and what a wonderful journey it's been. Thank you, my dear friend.

THE WORKSHOPPERS

To the beautiful girls who've made the trip to Bangalow to attend one of my workshops – this is for you.

MY COLLEAGUES

My lovely team, past and present, at the Little Cottage Studio – I'm so grateful you give me the support and structure I need to get things done. Nicky McLaughlin – for your boundless energy and support over many a cuppa. Sophie Saks – for your drive, vision and attention to every little detail. Charlotte Vermeersch – for your gorgeous youthful energy, always delivered with a smile.

FAMILY

My mother – always the voice of reason – for inspiring me to make home my life. And last but never least, my beautiful family – Michael, Inez and Joe – for giving me a raison d'être and the freedom to fly. I love you so very much.

Index

forming backdrop and
  framework 57, 58
and home's architectural
  style 57
floor coverings
  carpet 73
  tiles 57, 74–5
  timber 57, 73
  see also rugs
floor lamps 147, 151
floor plan 45
  creating 46–7
  ease of movement 46
  experimenting with 47–8
  lifestyle considerations 47, 50
floral fabric 133
flowers 176
  complementing furnishings
    176
  feature flowers 173
  florists' foam 176
  as focus 173
  foliage 176
  keeping fresh 176
  large arrangements 173
  simple arrangements 173, 176
  vases 173
fluorescent lighting 156
formal fabrics 130
formal room
  floor plan for 50
  furniture for 50
free-form fabric pattern 132
furniture
  and architecture of home 104
  bedroom 116
  buying 6
  choosing 104
  for formal room 50
  functional 104
  for greeting space 50
  living room 107–10
  making it fit 104
  for over-sized space 50
  placing against walls 50
  in proportion to room 45, 46
  for relaxed room 50
  for small space 50
  see also specific items
furniture suppliers 202

G

glamorous fabrics 129
glass mosaic tiles 74
gloss paint 67
green (colour) 84, 95
greeting space
  avoiding clutter 50
  floor plan for 50
  furniture for 50

grey (colour) 98
grid paper 9

H

halogen lighting 156
hemp fabrics 127
hessian fabrics 129
high ceilings, paint for 68
home office 3, 4, 116

J

jacquards, patterned 130
jute fabrics 127, 130

K

kitchen
  lighting 156
  splashback tiles 74
  wallpaper linings 61
knitted woolly furnishings 127

L

laminate floorboards 73
lamps
  bases 154
  floor 147, 151
  table 110, 147, 154–5
lampshades 151, 154–5
laundry tiles 74
layers of decorating 15
leather 127
library 4
light globes
  for bathroom 156
  bright white 156
  energy-efficient 156
  fluorescent 156
  halogens 156
  for kitchen 156
  yellowish light 156
light spaces, paint for 68
lighting, artificial
  architectural 147, 155
  candlelight 155
  chandeliers 154
  decorative 147, 155
  downlights 147, 151
  pendant 147, 151, 154
  shades 151, 154
  suppliers 202
  wall lights 147, 155
  see also lamps
lighting, natural 147, 148–50
  see also blinds; curtains
lime wash paints 70

linen cupboard 60
linen fabrics 126, 127, 129, 130
lists and schedules 9
living room
  furniture 107–10
  how it's used 107
long-lasting fabric 121
loose coverings 124

M

magazine and picture collection
  common thread in 25
  filing and organising 25
  scanning cuttings 8
  see also mood board
mantels, paint for 67
matt paint 67
memories and decorating 16
metallic paints 67
mirrors
  in confined space 168
  decorative frames 168
  grouping 168
  mixing sizes 168
modern geometric fabric 132
mood board
  backing for 32
  balancing elements 32
  and concept 34
  creating a concept 34
  playing with colour 29–32, 34
  textures 34
  virtual 32
mouldings, paint for 68

N

natural lighting 147, 148–50

O

online searches 36
orange (colour) 84, 92
organic fabric pattern 132
Osborne & Little wallpaper 58
ottomans, fabrics for 134
over-colour 34
over-sized space
  floor plan 50
  furniture 50
  paint choices 68

P

paint colour
  on 'backdrop' walls 63
  beginning with one wall 64

colour charts 63
colour chips 63–4
creating moods 63
fan deck or booklet 64
to feature walls 63
and light in room 64
sample pots 64
tones 63
paint finishes and textures
  cement 67, 70
  gloss 67
  matt or flat 67
  metallic 67
  satin or semi-gloss 67
  textured 67
  wiping clean 67
paint formulations
  acrylic 70
  eco-friendly 70
  enamel 70
  lime wash 70
  wood wash 70
paint suppliers 201
paint to highlight or disguise
  cornices 68
  dark spaces 68
  doors 68, 70
  high ceiling 68
  light space 68
  low ceiling 68
  mouldings 68
  oversized spaces 68
  skirting boards 68
  small room 68
  walls 63–7
pendant lights 147, 151, 154
photographs
  before and after 8
  filing 8
  for inspiration 8
  and styling 190
  trimming 9
pink (colour) 96
pinking shears 9
piping 124
plantation shutters 148, 150
playroom, wallpaper for 58
pleated and gathered skirts 124
porcelain tiles 74
pot plants
  blending with indoor scheme
    178
  choosing 178
  placing 178
  pots for 178–9
pressed metal on walls 70
  suppliers 204
primary colours 84
purple (colour) 84, 96

Featured artworks and products

p. vii – Erik Buch Bar Stool in kitchen; **p. 5** – Hyannis Port desk from Ligne Roset, rug by Madeline Weinrib, photograph by Julie Blackmon; **p. 11** – artwork *Waiting to Go* by Anna Cayzer; **p. 14** – Bertoia Large Diamond Chair; **p. 16** – artwork *Fading Memory* by Potts; **p. 17** – Lletteras I Tipos wallpaper by Funkis; **p. 20** – Shadow Floral wallpaper in Dusty Turquoise by Florence Broadhurst, Thonet Café Daum Settee; **p. 21** – artwork *Will You Meet Me in a Silent World?* by Hilary Herrmann; **p. 22** – Palm Leaves wallpaper by Cole & Son; **p. 23** – Tolix Tabouret stool from Thonet, artwork *Dora in a Landscape Without a Hat* by Jodie Hopkins; **p. 25** – artworks *The Owl* by Kim Amos and *High Rise* by Montgomery; **p. 26** – orange Tom Dixon Jack Light on floor; **p. 38** – Eames DSW Dining Chairs; **p. 40** – Tara/Grove Garden wallpaper by Osborne & Little in entrance, Stradivari wallpaper by Osborne & Little in dining room, Jarlathdan Regency chair in entrance (see also p. 100); **p. 49** – sofa by Profiles (NYC), armchairs by Pal + Smith (NYC), floor rug by The Rug Company, artwork by Anne Siems; **p. 56** – 'Pathé Marconi La Voix de son Maitre' poster by Bernard Villemot from Mark Tuckey; **p. 59** – Lily wallpaper by Cole & Son, Arteriors Coral Branch Table Lamps; **p. 62** – Louis Poulsen pendant light, Artek stools; **p. 65** – curtain in antique Balinese fabric; **p. 74** – tile samples from Jatana Interiors; **p. 76** – Catherine 9-drawer Mirrored Chest from Bungalow 5 (NYC); **p. 80** – artwork *Colo River* by Josh Yeldham, The Cranes and Japanese Bamboo fabrics by Florence Broadhurst on ottoman and sofa cushions, George Nelson Bubble Floor Lamp, Vincent Sheppard Butterfly armchairs; **p. 82** – artwork *Gone Thongin* by Potts; **p. 93** – Meurice light fitting by Robert Abbey; **p. 94** – curtain in Wattle Sunny Furnishing Fabric from Cloth, Alone in the Paddy Field fabric from No Chintz on armchair, Vincent Sheppard Chester Armchair sprayed to order (in corner); **p. 99** – Le Klint table lamp from Funkis; **p. 100** – Stradivari wallpaper by Osborne & Little, 1970s abstract bronze sculpture from Dana John, Large Ruhlmann chandelier from Circa Lighting (NYC), Philippe Starck Victoria Ghost Chairs in Crystal from Kartell, table bases from Machine Age with plexi tabletop made to order; **p. 105** – Lily wallpaper by Cole & Son, painting on side wall by Susan Kertesz; **p. 106** – Baxter sofa from Jonathan Adler, Haeger Potteries White Oval Ceramic Table Lamp, Plexi-Craft Waterfall Cocktail Table, chair from Pal + Smith upholstered in Passiflora fabric by Missoni; **p. 109** – artwork *Deathstar* by Mark de Jong; **p. 111** – George Nelson Bubble Lamp, Aristoc dining stools by Grant Featherstone; **p. 112** – Tolix A Chair from Thonet; **p. 115** – Tholix Tabouret stools from Thonet; **p. 118** – table from Assemblage (NYC), chairs from Baker Knapp & Tubbs (NYC), Passiflora fabric by Missoni on blind, Jean de Merry chandelier and wall sconce; **p. 122** – photos by Max Creasy; **p. 123** – Jardan Chair upholstered in Kenzo fabric, Japanese Bamboo fabric by Florence Broadhurst on floor cushions, Anna Castelli Ferrieri Componibili at front left; **p. 128** – antique settee upholstered in fabric from Osborne & Little, Bracelet Chair by Barbara Barry/Henredon, Porcupine Quill Mirror from Horchow, rug by Madeline Weinrib; **p. 131** – curtain in Jarman Tenda fabric by Missoni; **p. 149** – Asuka wallpaper by Osborne & Little on pendant lights; **p. 153** – Artek stools, Louis Poulsen pendant light over sink, Le Klint pendant light at left from Funkis; **p. 157** – Bertoia Bar Stools; **p. 158** – Gardenia wallpaper in New Chevalier Blue and Akira Yellow by Florence Broadhurst, Vincent Sheppard Butterfly armchair; **p. 162** – artwork framed Camilla Engman tea towel from Third Drawer Down; **p. 165** – artworks clockwise from top left: hand-coloured etching by Markus Lüpertz, pencil drawing by Markus Lüpertz, two-panel piece by Mitchell English, abstract by Roy Churcher and painting by Ines English; **p. 166** – Farfalla wallpaper by Nina Campbell, circus drawings by Alexander Calder; **p. 167** – painting *Skull* by Mitchell English; **p. 169** – Shadow Floral wallpaper in Dusty Turquoise by Florence Broadhurst, Thonet Café Daum Settee; **p. 181** – artworks by Hilary Herrmann; **p. 183** – armchairs by Pal + Smith, floor rug by The Rug Company; **p. 186** – armchairs by Vincent Sheppard, Petal table by Richard Schultz, painting *Safety in the Dark* by Hilary Herrmann; **p. 191** – Eames chair and footstool; **p. 193** – John Derian Silver Moroccan Poufs, artwork *Praia Piquinia* by Christian Chaize.

Published in the United States by Potter Style, an imprint of the
Crown Publishing Group, a division of Random House, Inc., New York.
www.crownpublishing.com
www.clarksonpotter.com

POTTER STYLE and colophon is a registered trademark of Random House, Inc.

Originally published in Australia by Lantern, an imprint of the Penguin Group,
Australia, Melbourne, in 2012.

Library of Congress Cataloging-in-Publication Data
Fricke, Shannon.
   How to decorate/Shannon Fricke; photographs by Prue Ruscoe.
   Includes index.
1. Interior decoration. I. Title

NK2115.F69 2013
747--dc23   2012050818

ISBN 978-0-385-34507-1
eISBN 978-0-385-34515-6

Printed in China

Design and illustrations by Emily O'Neill © Penguin Group (Australia)
Cover design and illustrations by Emily O'Neill

10 9 8 7 6 5 4 3 2 1

First American Edition